The Craft of Writing

THOMAS ELLIOTT BERRY

McGraw-Hill Book Company

New York • St. Louis • San Francisco • London • Düsseldorf
Kuala Lumpur • Mexico • Montreal • Panama • São Paulo
Sydney • Toronto • Johannesburg • New Delhi • Singapore

Acknowledgments

Henry B. Arthur, "On Rivalry in the Marketplace," from *Harvard Business Review*, October 1972. Used by permission of *Harvard Business Review*.

Jules Backman, excerpt from *Advertising and Competition*, New York University Press, 1967. Reprinted by permission of the New York University Press from *Advertising and Competition* by Jules Backman. Copyright © 1967 by New York University.

"Insurance that Pays the Dentist's Bills." Reprinted by permission from *Changing Times*, the Kiplinger Magazine (September 1972 issue). Copyright 1972 by The Kiplinger Washington Editors, Inc., 1729 H Street, N.W., Washington, D.C. 20006.

Carlton B. Lees, "Editorial" in *Horticulture*, October 1972. Reprinted by permission of *Horticulture* published by the Massachusetts Horticulture Society.

Gene Logsdon, "He Tackled a Giant and Won," *Farm Journal* May 1973. Reprinted by special permission from the May 1973 issue of *Farm Journal*. © 1973 by *Farm Journal, Inc.*

7 8 9 10 FGFG 8 7

Library of Congress Cataloging in Publication Data

Berry, Thomas Elliott.
    The craft of writing.

    (McGraw-Hill paperbacks)
        1. English language—Rhetoric.   I. Title.
PE1408.B483   808'.042   74-3498
ISBN 0-07-005051-1

Preface

This book is intended to serve as a guide for the person who seeks to improve his writing. It is a collection of the fundamental lessons to be mastered in any carefully devised plan to develop acceptable written expression.

Broadly speaking, the book aims to provide answers to the two all-important questions: What is effective writing? How can I acquire that kind of writing?

All material has been divided into three parts: The Elements of Writing, The Forms of Writing, and The Writing Process. These classifications represent the natural division of material to be covered in any serious attempt to improve writing. The entire book, therefore, should be viewed as a series of logically arranged lessons or an arrangement of successive stages through which every writer must pass in his or her quest of better expression.

Within each of the three main parts, subdivisions have been made to assist the reader in examining the material more profitably and more comfortably.

Part I begins with the use of the word and then treats successively the sentence and the paragraph. With each discussion you, the reader, should try to correlate the matter under consideration with the material that preceded it. Only by understanding words, for example, can you truly understand the sentence, and only by understanding the sentence can you understand the paragraph. Thus when you finish the section, you should see each point as a foundation stone for the whole activity of writing competently.

You should follow a similar procedure in Part II. This section discusses the four main types of writing—description, narration, exposition, and argument—and once again, the order of treatment rests on natural considerations. Description is handled first because it is a bedrock element in the other three forms. Narration follows because a writer must grasp its inherent nature as a prelude to understanding exposition and argument. And exposition precedes argument because the latter is essentially an offshoot of the former.

Hence in this section, as everywhere else, you should see every discussion as a basis for understanding the material that follows.

Part III deals with the specific aspects of the actual writing process. It handles each of the four stages of writing—thinking, planning, writing, and revising in their chronological and hence logical order. Throughout, it demonstrates how the four parts of the writing process are like the four phases of the furniture refinisher's work (cleaning, sanding, undercoating, and final coating), and it shows how the quality of the final product is in direct proportion to all that has preceded.

As you study the illustrative material in this book, remember always that you must strive to develop sound critical abilities. Remember that before you can write well, you must be able to recognize good writing. This statement is true because a sound critical judgment discloses the direction in which you point your efforts. Equally important, it enables you to judge your own writing competently.

Finally, remember that writing is a complex skill. And like all such skills, it can be developed only by practice under proper conditions.

The mere act of writing will not make you a writer. Always, you must write with the aim of doing your very best, with the thought that every piece of writing must exceed the last, with your sights on constant improvement. Then you will be practicing under proper conditions.

West Chester, Pennsylvania   T.E.B.

Contents

Preface   v

Part One: **The elements of writing**   1

   1.   Your writing style   3

   2.   Right words for emphasis   7

       Limited-meaning words   7
       Unusual words   9
       Specialized terminology   11
       Deliberate phrases   12
       Original words and phrases   14
       Synonyms   15

   3.   Writing sentences   19

       Basic patterns   19
       Grammatical element patterns   20
       Variety of sentence lengths   24
       Fundamental stylistic techniques   24

4. Rhetorical devices   33

Analogy   33
Allusion   36
Antithesis   37
Paradox   38
Balance   39
Repetition   41
Restatement   42
Foreign phrases   43
Direct quotation   44
Understatement   46
Unexpected turn   46
Intensifiers   48
Figures of speech   49

5. Humor, mild satire, and parody   53

Humor   53
Mild satire   55
Parody   57

6. Undesirable conditions in expression   59

Jargon   59
Purple prose   60
Trite expressions   61
Platitudes   61
Euphemisms   62
Overstatement   62
Temporary suspension   63
Ephemeral words and phrases   64

7. The nature of the paragraph   67

Function   67

Content   71
Arrangement   72

8. Attributes of the paragraph   75

Completeness   75
Capability   76
Unity   78
Coherence   78
Fluency   79
Pace   81
Proportion   85
Atmosphere   86
Rhythm   89

9. The structure of the paragraph   91

Thesis sentence   91
Implied thesis   93
Question and answer   94
Definition   95
Analysis   96
Comparison or contrast   98
Successive steps   100
Point-by-point development   101
Effect to cause   102
Cause to effect   103
The unusual stylistic device   104

Part Two: The forms of writing   107

10. Description   109

11. Narration   115

12. Exposition   125

Definition   130
Analysis   132
Clarification   134
Comparison   135
Explanation of relationships   136

13. Argument   139

Collecting evidence for argument   140
Preparing the case in argument   143

Part Three: The writing process   151

14. Formulating your thoughts   153

15. Planning your paper   157

Narration   157
Description   165
Exposition   173
Argument   178

16. From rough draft to final copy   183

Writing the rough draft   183
Revising for the final copy   184

Appendix: Rules for the use of the comma   193

Part One

The elements of writing

1.

Your writing style

The manner in which a writer characteristically expresses himself is termed his "style." Broadly speaking, style includes word choice, rhetorical devices, sentence structures, and every other pattern of expression—all of which are employed in the distinctly individual manner of the particular user. Thus we say that Dr. Samuel Johnson has a Latinate style, Washington Irving a leisurely style, Henry James an involved style, and John Steinbeck a direct style. We may also speak of literary styles, business letter styles, and journalistic styles.

If you want to improve your writing, you must begin by appraising your style. This means that you must assess your choice of words, sentence structure, and general mode of expression with the aim of learning where and how to improve; and you must repeat this appraisal every time you write.

When you appraise your writing, remember that, just as one master painter's technique may be quite different from that of another, sharply different styles of writing can be equally effective. You should aim at improving your own natural expression to achieve your greatest possible power, clarity, and appeal.

To appreciate how effective a variety of styles can be, study the following examples of strong writing:

- On a hill by the Mississippi where Chippewas camped two generations ago, a girl stood in relief against the cornflower blue of Northern sky. She saw no Indians now; she saw flour-mills and the blinking windows of skyscrapers in Minneapolis and St. Paul. Nor was she thinking of squaws and portages, and the Yankee fur-traders whose shadows were all about her. She was meditating upon walnut fudge, the plays of Brieux, the reasons why heels run over, and the fact that the chemistry instructor had stared at the new coiffure which concealed her ears.   [Sinclair Lewis, *Main Street*, 1920.]

Lewis' style in this passage is noteworthy for the choice of words and selection of detail, and the ease with which the sentences flow. Note especially the force Lewis gains by contrasting the past with the present and by recounting the girl's thoughts against the backdrop of the industrial might of the two cities.

● I read about it in the paper, in the subway, on my way to work. I read it, and I couldn't believe it, and I read it again. Then perhaps I just stared at it, at the newsprint spelling out his name, spelling out the story. I stared at it in the swinging lights of the subway car, and in the faces and bodies of the people, and in my own face, trapped in the darkness which roared outside.   [James Baldwin, "Sonny's Blues," 1957.]

In this paragraph, Baldwin employs effectively the style of a bewildered man reacting to an incident that has shocked him. Through natural and fluent expression, coupled with uninhibited presentation of the man's impressions, Baldwin achieves unusual power and appeal.

● ### It Was Invisible, as Always

They had begun to vote in the villages of New Hampshire at midnight, as they always do, seven and a half hours before the candidate rose. His men had canvassed Hart's Location in New Hampshire days before, sending his autographed picture to each of the twelve registered voters in the village. They knew that they had five votes certain there, that Nixon had five votes certain—and that two were still undecided. Yet it was worth the effort, for Hart's Location's results would be the first flash of news on the wires to greet millions of voters as they opened their morning papers over coffee. But from there on it was unpredictable—invisible. [Theodore H. White, *The Making of the President 1960*, 1961.]

The attraction of this paragraph arises from the directness with which the author speaks. His sentences are simple and pointed; they give the reader a clear understanding of the message on the first reading. The selection also achieves a smoothly flowing quality that adds a pleasing tone of reminiscence.

● When the youth awoke it seemed to him that he had been asleep for a thousand years, and he felt sure that he opened his eyes upon an unexpected world. Gray mists were slowly shifting before the first efforts of the sunrays. An impending splendor could be seen in the eastern sky. An icy dew had chilled his face, and immediately upon arousing he curled farther down into his blankets. He stared for a while at the leaves overhead, moving in a heraldic wind of the day. [Stephen Crane, *The Red Badge of Courage*, 1895.]

This passage is remarkable for the amount of significant detail Crane has packed into each sentence. As the reader follows the description, he derives a clear understanding of the scene because of the writer's ability to cast a picture-making sentence through his use of unusual words and his presentation of just the right detail at just the right time.

● We admit that in many places and in ordinary times the defendants in saying all that was said in the circular would have been within their constitutional rights. But the character of every act depends upon the circumstances in which it is done. The most stringent protection of free speech would not protect a man in falsely shouting fire in a theatre and causing a panic. It does not even protect a man from an injunction against uttering words that may have all the effect of force. The question in every case is whether the words used are used in such circumstances and are of such a nature as to create a clear and present danger that they will bring about the substantive evils that Congress has a right to prevent. It is a question of proximity and degree. When a nation is at war many things that might be said in time of peace are such a hindrance to its effort that their utterance will not be endured so long as men fight and that no Court could regard them as protected by any constitutional right. It seems to be admitted that if an actual obstruction of the recruiting service were proved, liability for words that produced that effect might be enforced. The statute of 1917 in sec. 4 punishes conspiracies to obstruct as well as actual obstruction. If the act, (speaking, or circulating a paper) its tendency and the intent with which it is done are the same, we perceive no ground for saying that success alone warrants making the act a crime.   [Oliver Wendell Holmes, Jr., *Schenck v. U.S.*, 1919.]

This paragraph, which stands as one of the most important judicial guidelines for freedom of expression, is outstanding for its clarity of statement. Nowhere is there any doubt about the meaning, and nowhere is there any serious impediment to smoothly flowing discourse. Reflect especially on the second and the third sentences and on such phrases as "clear and present danger" and "substantive evils."

2.

Right words for emphasis

To appreciate the importance of the words that you use in your writing, remember these two statements: (1) a single word in a sentence can determine the essential meaning of the entire sentence, and (2) the difference between mediocre writing and excellent writing is often no more than a difference in choice of words.

The following classifications can serve as guidelines in your all-important search for the right or strong word.

Limited-meaning words

General-meaning words, such as "dog," "house," and "sing," create broad, nonspecific ideas or images. Limited-meaning words, such as "collie," "bungalow," "trill," create more restricted, hence more precise ideas or images. The use of more specific, limited-meaning words will make your sentence more emphatic. Consider, for example, the simple statement:

o   The horse jumped over the barrier.

This sentence lacks the emphasis of the statement:

●   The palomino eased over the barrier.

7

Similarly, in each of the four pairs of sentences below, the second sentence is the more emphatic because of the presence of limited-meaning words.

○   The football player *pushed* his way through the *opposing* line.

●   The *halfback bulled* his way through the *charging* line.

○   The lawyer *looked at* the man's *face*.

●   The lawyer *studied* the *stranger's expression*.

○   Over the city's *houses* a *large* eagle *flew* toward *less populated areas*.

●   Over the *silhouette* of the city, a *giant* eagle *soared* toward the *distant forest*.

○   *Large* waves were *rolling* against the wharf, *straining* the *not-too-strong* underpinning.

●   *Massive* waves were *pounding* the wharf, *threatening* to tear out the *frail* underpinning.

The importance of selecting the correct limited-meaning word can be appreciated by examining a thesaurus or similar listing. Note, for instance, the listing for the limited-meaning noun *booty* taken from Roget's *Thesaurus*. What shades of meanings do you see in these apparent synonyms: spoil, loot, plunder, prize, swag, boodle, pickings, *spolia opima*, prey, stolen goods? As you can see, the English language is rich in limited-meaning words. They await selection by the discerning writer.

In the following passages, you will see how well-known writers have used limited-meaning words to strengthen their writing. To assist you in studying these examples, the limited-meaning words are italicized.

●   Old Henry and his wife Phoebe were as fond of each other as it is possible for old people to be who have nothing else in this life to be fond of. He was a thin old man, seventy when she died, a *queer, crotchety* person with *coarse gray-black* hair and beard, quite *straggly* and *unkempt*. He looked at you out of *dull, fishy, watery* eyes that had *deep-brown crow's feet* at the sides. His clothes were *aged* and *angular* and *baggy*, standing out at the pockets, not fitting about the neck, *protuberant* and worn at elbow and knee.   [Theodore Dreiser, "The Lost Phoebe," 1916.]

• The man who now watched the fire was of a different order, and troubled himself with no thoughts save the very few that were *requisite* to his business. At frequent intervals, he flung back the *clashing weight* of the *iron* door, and, turning his face from the *insufferable* glare, thrust in *huge* logs of oak, or stirred the *immense* brands with a long pole. Within the furnace were seen the *curling* and *riotous* flames, and the burning marble, almost *molten* with the intensity of heat; while without, the reflection of the fire *quivered* on the dark *intricacy* of the *surrounding* forest and showed in the foreground a *bright* and *ruddy* picture of the hut, the spring beside its door, the *athletic* and *coal-begrimed* figure of the lime-burner, and the *half-frightened* child, *shrinking* into the protection of his father's shadow.   [Nathaniel Hawthorne, "Ethan Brand," 1850.]

• The city's deep streets are hot as the *funnels* of a stove, the bedrooms like *bakeries*. From cabs parked on street corners the *high* voices of baseball commentators *rattle* out from portable radios, and all there is of the driver *slumped* inside is one *fat, shirtless* arm over the door. The Elevated *bangs* past tenements with all their windows open, *dank* laundry over the ledges, and *vast* women *shuffling* around inside carrying frying pans or little flower-pots. You see old men sitting on the stoops, and babies *spilling* over the sidewalks, and cars *hooting* at little boys *darting* into the roadway carrying baseball bats.   [Alistair Cooke, "No Sympathy for Apathy," 1952.]

Unusual words

An *unusual word* is one that is seldom encountered or that is not normally used to express a thought like one you may be trying to convey. Properly employed, the unusual word achieves emphasis through novelty.

The following examples show how effective the use of the unusual word (italicized, in each case) can be.

- "What does he mean by Malabar?" asked the *frozen-hearted* mother. [D. H. Lawrence, "The Rocking-Horse Winner," 1933.]

- The sun, *driving* straight down, *stung* with its rays. [John Steinbeck, *Grapes of Wrath*, 1939.]

- Truman was *hagridden* by a long, apparently stalemated Asian war. [*Time*, April 12, 1968.]

- He had a broad, quite cold, *wind-gnawed* face... [William Faulkner, "Spotted Horses," 1931.]

- A *singular disadvantage* of the sea lies in the fact that after successfully surmounting one wave you discover that there is another behind it just as *important*... [Stephen Crane, "The Open Boat," 1898.]

- *Grayly* the sky promised more snow, but now, at the end of the day following his collapse in the chapel, it was melting. [J. F. Powers, "Lions, Harts, Leaping Does," 1933.]

You can appreciate further the value of unusual words by reading the two passages presented below. The first is an account of changing of the horses on a stagecoach as it would be given by a writer indifferent to the value of the unusual word. The second passage is the work of Mark Twain, one of America's best writers.

- We jumped out in our untidy clothing. The driver threw his reins out on the ground, looked around and stretched himself, took off his large gloves with great care and affectation—without even noticing the dozen or so people who were greeting him and asking how he was feeling. Also, five or six unkempt station-keepers and hostlers were unhitching the horses and bringing new horses out of the stables, meanwhile trying to please the driver by being ready to help him in any way by doing little favors.

● We jumped out in *undress uniform.* The driver tossed his gathered reins out on the ground, gaped and stretched complacently, drew off his heavy buckskin gloves with great deliberation and *insufferable dignity*—taking not the slightest notice of a dozen solicitous inquiries after his health, and *humbly facetious* and *flattering accostings,* and *obsequious tenders* of service, from five or six *hairy* and half-civilized station-keepers and hostlers who were nimbly unhitching our steeds and bringing the fresh team out of the stables... [*Roughing It,* 1872.]

Specialized terminology

In specialized fields, there is always a nomenclature or vocabulary that you must master if you are to speak or write knowledgeably in that field.

For instance, medicine has such terms as "endocrine," "hepatitis," and "subcutaneous." Law has, among many others, such terms as "misdemeanor," "plaintiff," and "tort." In chemistry, as every student knows, there are such terms as "alkali," "hydrochloric," and "saline."

Usually, the careful writer has no difficulty with unfamiliar situations and terms in a specialized field, because he checks before he writes. However, the best of writers must beware of words in common parlance (those used by people in their daily lives) that have specialized meanings within a particular field.

The terms "insult" and "inspire," for example, have specialized meanings in medicine. The terms "plead" and "argue" have specialized meanings in law. The terms "base" and "effervesce" have specialized meanings in chemistry. Therefore, to avoid error, you must exercise care in using terms with common and specialized meanings when writing in a specialized field.

In addition, you must recognize a closely related truth: A writer gains force by using precise rather than loose terminology. Note, for example, the pairs of sentences below. The first sentence of each pair uses loose phraseology; the second employs specialized terminology to express the same thought more precisely.

○   My neighbor has a large *group of bee hives*.

●   My neighbor has a large *apiary*.

○   The official signalled that it was *time to start playing again*.

●   The head linesman signalled *time-in*.

○   An *eye doctor* was examining the injured man's eye.

●   An *ophthalmologist* was examining the injured man's eye.

○   A *specialist in psychological testing* was studying the test results.

●   A *psychometrist* was studying the test results.

○   The dog looked like a *big cream-colored Irish setter*.

●   The dog was a *golden retriever*.

○   A *faculty member carrying a baton* was leading the academic procession.

●   The *senior member of the English Department* was serving as *chief marshall* for the academic procession.

Deliberate phrases

Often, by reflecting sufficiently, a writer can evolve an original phrase that evokes a world of thought. Such a phrase, even upon superficial examination, drives home a thought resoundingly. These so-called deliberate phrases are likely to appear in the works of our best thinkers as they attempt to express a far-reaching concept in a single phrase.

You would do well to study such phrases whenever you meet them. They are not beyond your reach as a writer, if you give sufficient thought to the questions or ideas you are raising.

Here are a few examples in which the deliberate phrases have been italicized:

●   The First Amendment, then, is not the *guardian of unregulated talkativeness.* [Alexander Meiklejohn, "The Rulers and the Ruled," 1948.]

- No, I distrust Great Men. They produce a *desert of uniformity* around them and often a pool of blood too, and I always feel a little man's pleasure when they come a cropper. [E. M. Forster, "What I Believe," 1951.]

- ...no more pernicious doctrine has ever found its way into American law or into popular acceptance than this doctrine of guilt by association. . . . Why is there no *doctrine of innocence by association*? [Henry Steele Commager, *Freedom, Loyalty, Dissent*, 1953.]

- But if we are to revive and recover, and are to go forward again, we must not look for the root of the trouble in our adversaries. We must look for it in ourselves. We must rid ourselves of the *poison of self-pity.* [Walter Lippmann, "The Shortage in Education," 1962.]

- [Historian Henry] Adams brought to the exposition his great gift for *purposeful brooding.* [Norman Cousins, "Time to Think," 1955.]

- Truth *has its own claims,* especially in a democratic society. If an institution [the Supreme Court] cannot survive disclosures about its internal dynamics, then serious questions are raised about the legitimacy of that institution . . . [Alan Dershowitz, "The Ultimate Fraternity," 1980.]

- Middle-aged men must beware the dangers inherent in becoming *weekend athletes.*

- The best way to stay ahead in the never ending game of driving on the nation's highways is to *drive defensively.*

- Some people develop a *pathological resistance* to change.

- To be well dressed, a man must learn to wear quality clothing with a *studied carelessness.*

- The President of the United States was engaging in *brinksmanship diplomacy.*

- The barber shop habitué is invariably an *authority by self-proclamation.*

- Large universities tend to provide an *assembly line education* that creates standardized products.

Original words and phrases

On some occasions, a writer can obtain a powerful effect by departing from standard vocabulary, by taking liberties with an established form, or by using unorthodox phraseology.

Note the force gained by the use of this device, italicized in the following examples.

- A more fundamental cause of violent activism is the presence on most campuses of large universities of thousands of young, disoriented, and *goalless* young people.   [Neil H. Jacoby, *The Center Magazine*, May 1969.]

- As the literary heritage of the Beat Generation . . . we are left the *unreadable un-novels* of Kerouac and the first part of "Howl."   [John Ciardi, "Epitaph for the Dead Beats," 1963.]

- And so what I am trying to make you understand is that every contemporary writer has to find out what is the *inner time-sense of his contemporariness.*   [Gertrude Stein, "How Writing is Written," 1935.]

- We believe that a magazine is essentially a reading, rather than a viewing, experience. In this sense, we will publish for a *readership rather than a flippership.*   [Norman Cousins, advertisement in *Time* for his magazine *World*, April 3, 1972.]

- Current writers have a strong tendency to dwell excessively on their own thoughts, emotions, and ego. "*First personism* has become an epidemic contagion."   [Herbert Gold, "On Epidemic First Personism," *The Atlantic*, August 1971.]

- [The English language has] the *broncolike ability* . . . to throw whoever leaps *cocksurely* into the saddle.   [E. B. White, *The Second Tree from the Corner*, 1951.]

- The rise in censorship is in part due, I believe, to the *concern of the half-educated for the well-being of the quarter-educated.* [Fred B. Millett, "The Vigilantes," *AAUP Bulletin*, Spring 1954.]

The following sentences illustrate student uses of the original word or phrase.

The girls down the hall had a bad case of *dormitoryitis.*

Economics was a difficult course because of the *dearth of curve flatteners to offset the curve raisers.*

Our botany professor should be designated *"Robot in Residence."*

By all means, experiment with language in your writing, but do not merely copy the original phrases of others. Yesterday's original phrase often becomes today's cliché.

Synonyms

The term "synonym" denotes a word having essentially the same meaning as another. For example, "bravery" and "valor" are considered synonyms.

The synonym is especially useful in avoiding monotony of expression. If you were to write,

○ The aspirant must practice *diligently*, study *diligently*, and work *diligently*.

you would tire your reader. You can avoid that undesirable effect by writing,

● The aspirant must practice *diligently*, study *thoroughly*, and work *unceasingly*.

A second and equally important function of synonyms is this: the capable use of synonyms invariably contributes to strong writing. The writer, for instance, who says in his first draft,

○ The pipe smoke *rose in the air.*

can improve his sentence by using synonymous expressions:

● The pipe smoke *curled skyward.*

You must be careful about substituting synonyms for a word because: (1) Synonymous terms may have slightly different meanings. For instance, the connotation of "valor" is slightly loftier than "bravery." Similarly, "working industriously" conveys a more intense meaning than "working hard."

You must be aware of such differences when you use a thesaurus. Therefore, do not purchase a thesaurus with the thought that the matter of synonyms is now automatically under control. The thesaurus can tell you little or nothing of connotations and fine shades of meaning. Its strength is that it can help you to find possible synonyms; to select the right one you should be guided by your own knowledge of English and the definitions listed in a good dictionary.

(2) Many scientific terms—*nitrogen, hydrogen,* and *phosphorous,* for example—have no synonyms. Such terms must be repeated or replaced with pronouns where possible.

To appreciate the power carefully selected synonyms can add to your writing, examine the passages below. The writers represented have been quite successful in finding synonyms for commonplace words and phrases. Instead of using the trite phraseology of much of our everyday speech, they have sought out synonymous terms (italicized). The result is a refreshing atmosphere of originality that increases the impact of the selections.

- In the past few years a good many persons have been lining up, like *sailors* at a shooting gallery, to *draw a bead* on the various media of mass communication. [Theodore Peterson, "Why the Mass Media Are That Way," 1963.]

To see how capably this writer has chosen the right word from a group of synonyms, simply substitute "patrons" for "sailors" and "aim guns" for "draw a bead." Notice how the sentence droops. Quickly put back Peterson's original words.

- The guard *eyed* us and our clothes with *sullen distaste.* [Loren Eiseley, *The Unexpected Universe,* 1969.]

Once again, the force of the right word chosen from a group of synonyms can be appreciated by the process of substitution. Try to find better words than "eyed" and "sullen distaste."

● ... And now to end with an important point: my own performances upon the piano. They grow worse yearly, but never will I give them up. For one thing, they *compel me to attend*—no *wool-gathering* or *thinking myself clever* here—and they *drain off* all *non-musical matter*. For another thing, they teach me a little about construction. I see what becomes of a phrase, how it is transformed or returned, sometimes *bottom upward*, and get some notion of the relation of keys. Playing Beethoven, as I generally do, I grow familiar with his tricks, his impatience, his sudden *softnesses*, his dropping of a tragic theme one semitone, his love, when tragic, for the key of C minor, and his *aversion* to the key of B major. This gives me a physical approach to Beethoven which cannot be gained through the *slough of "appreciation."* Even when people play as badly as I do, they should continue: it helps them to listen.   [E. M. Forster, "Not Listening to Music," 1939.]

This particular passage is representative of an almost instinctive ability to select the right or best words. Forster, like other highly respected writers, seems to have an easily accessible storehouse of synonyms from which to choose the best or strongest word, as shown by the italicized words.

3.

Writing the sentence

A carefully contrived, soundly executed sentence is a benchmark of competence. It indicates the writer's progression from a level of mediocrity or bare adequacy to a high level of proficiency. Therefore, you must develop your ability to write such a sentence.

To write finished sentences, you first must have at your fingertips a variety of sentence structures. Ideally, in every instance, you should be capable of employing the sentence structure that contributes most to the pleasing movement essential to effective expression—the movement that carries your reader along easily and comfortably from point to point as he receives your message.

Basic patterns

The first step in mastering an assortment of structures is to review the three basic sentence patterns you learned long ago.

The *simple sentence* is actually one independent clause. For example:

The outfielder tripped against the wall.

The *compound sentence* is composed of two independent clauses joined by a coordinating conjunction. For example,

The outfielder tripped against the wall, but he was not injured.

The *complex sentence* is composed of one dependent and one independent clause. For example,

Although the outfielder tripped against the wall, he was not injured.

Grammatical element patterns

After reviewing these basic structures, you should next think of sentence patterns that evolve from grammatical elements. Grammarians often use the term "element" to denote a word or group of words within a sentence that functions as a unit of thought.

By thinking of the principal elements identified by grammarians, you can obtain further insight into the art of writing effective sentences.

The most commonly recognized elements are presented below.

Introductory elements. An *introductory element* is a word or group of words employed to introduce a thought. In the sentence,

To summarize, this condition is clearly unsatisfactory.

the first two words constitute the introductory element. Other examples of introductory elements are: "however," "moreover," "nevertheless," "in short," "in brief," "in the final analysis," "therefore," and "all in all."

The introductory element is especially useful in effecting smooth transitions. It achieves a cohesive effect by showing the relationship between the thoughts preceding and following it. Note the passage below, for example:

● Because he was unsteady and unreliable, we simply could not employ him. *As a result*, we had to seek elsewhere.

In selecting introductory elements, you must be aware of triteness. Such elements as "to make a long story short," "for all intents and purposes," and "not to go around Robin's barn" have been worn thin by overuse. You would be well advised never to employ them.

Parenthetical elements. A *parenthetical element* is a word or group of words that creates the effect of an afterthought. A parenthetical element could well be placed in parentheses. Note the following:

Jimmy De Shong, *Heaven knows how*, passed his final exams.

My neighbor, *bless him*, begins to practice his trumpet at the crack of dawn.

One of my lodge brothers—*affectionately known as "Honest Abe"*—is a real card sharp.

A capable writer can frequently obtain a strong effect by using the parenthetical element. To appreciate this fact, study the parenthetical elements (italicized) in the sentences below, which have been taken from the writings of well known authors.

- Sergeant Peter, *young as he was*, had a great influence over his men.   [Joseph Conrad, "Prince Roman," 1912.]

- And she had that maddening habit of asking for just an inch more bread to finish what she had on her plate, and then, at the last mouthful, absent-mindedly—*of course it wasn't absent-mindedly*—taking another helping.   [Katherine Mansfield, "The Daughters of the Late Colonel," 1923.]

- Can we not take this sense of moral purpose—*so intolerable when it sets itself above the world, but so indomitable when it sets itself to a hard job*—and shape from it a tool with which the building of a new world can be done?   [Margaret Mead, "If We Are to Go On," 1964.]

- The greatness of Rome (*such is the language of the historian*) was founded on the rare and almost incredible alliance of virtue and of fortune.   [Edward Gibbon, *The Decline and Fall of the Roman Empire*, 1788.]

Absolute elements.   An *absolute element* is one that has no grammatical dependence on the rest of the sentence; that is, it stands apart.

> Snow gently falling on the trees in the garden, we stood before the fireplace in the study.
>
> His final exams all behind him, Sal sat on the front porch looking at nothing in particular.
>
> The car pulled onto the ferry, the radiator bubbling like a volcano.
>
> Dave, a little party hat atop his large head, lustily welcomed in the new year.

When used competently, the absolute element can be powerful. The great caution is to use it sparingly. It is somewhat like seasoning for food; it must be used in just the right way at just the right moment.

Appositives.   An *appositive* is a word or group of words employed to identify or enlarge upon a noun concept. For example, in the sentence,

> Mr. Baker, *owner of the store*, handled the transaction.

The phrase "owner of the store" is an appositive.

In attempting to point up expression, you will frequently find that a carefully designed appositive strengthens your writing considerably.

Examine the sentences below as they are written. Then read them without the italicized appositive. This procedure should convince you of the effectiveness of careful use of appositives.

● The teller, *a slight, emaciated man with a hangdog expression*, dutifully examined both sides of the check.

- Mrs. Hogan, *a mammoth woman with a quick Irish wit,* peered mischievously down her nose at the visitor.

- So after we had left Lausanne and gone down to Italy, I showed the racing story to O'Brien, *a gentle, shy man, pale, with pale blue eyes, and straight lanky hair he cut himself,* who lived then as a boarder in a monastery up above Rapallo.   [Ernest Hemingway, *A Moveable Feast,* 1964.]

- Mr. Tyser always looked tired. *A good little man, no harm in him, but at wit's end in dealing with noisy fools of boys.* [Richard Llewellyn, *How Green Was My Valley,* 1939.]

- While Robin deliberated of whom to inquire respecting his kinsman's dwelling, he was accosted by the innkeeper, *a little man in a stained white apron,* who had come to pay his professional welcome to the stranger.   [Nathaniel Hawthorne, "My Kinsman, Major Molineux," 1832.]

- The dying man himself was no longer to be duped by hope; he knew that he was done for, and he no longer cared. Rather, as if that knowledge had brought a new strength—*the immense and measureless strength that comes from resignation, and that has vanquished terror and despair*—Gant had already consigned himself to death, and now was waiting for it, without weariness or anxiety, and with a perfect and peaceful acquiescence. [Thomas Wolfe, *Of Time and the River,* 1935.]

Participial phrases. In the *participial phrase sentence,* the phrase generally occurs at the beginning of the sentence:

- *Walking up the long drive,* Hilda looked in vain for her purse.

However, the phrase can sometimes be placed effectively in other parts of the sentence:

- Hilda, *walking up the long drive,* looked in vain for her purse.

You must be careful in transposing this phrase to avoid an unintended or humorous meaning:

○ Hilda looked in vain for her purse, *walking up the long drive.*

Variety of sentence lengths

While the length of a sentence affects its ability to convey information or move a reader, there is no one correct length for all sentences. By writing sentences of different lengths, you can best keep the interest of your readers. Notice the effects gained in the paragraph below by composing sentences with varying numbers of words.

- Looking from one juror to the next, the judge seemed perplexed and disappointed. He seemed unable to understand how they could possibly have reached such a verdict in view of the overwhelming evidence to the contrary. Silent and defeated, he hung his head for a few seconds and then looked about the courtroom. He recognized the inevitable. There was no point in tongue-lashing this jury or striving to undo a settled fact.

One short sentence after another can make monotonous reading. Often two or more such sentences can be combined effectively. Study the following paragraph:

○ The smoke was rising from the chimney tops. It was a cold day. The sun was slowly sinking behind the distant trees. Everything began to look dark and ominous.

By combining sentences, you can obtain the following:

- The smoke was rising from the chimney tops on that very cold day as the sun slowly sank behind the distant trees, creating a dark and ominous atmosphere.

Fundamental stylistic techniques

In addition to the approaches already presented, you should master the techniques and devices discussed below.

Unusual placement of words. By placing a single word in an unusual or unconventional position, a writer can frequently obtain a startling impact.

Note how the second sentence in each of the pairs below is strengthened by moving one word or phrase to a less common position.

○ The judge waited impatiently for the roar of disapproval to subside.

● Impatiently, the judge waited for the roar of disapproval to subside.

○ The stunned leopard crouched on the ledge.

● The leopard, stunned, crouched on the ledge.

○ Vinson sagged, crestfallen as match point was scored.

● Vinson sagged as matchpoint was scored—crestfallen.

○ What does the word "friendship" really mean?

● Friendship. What does the word really mean?

○ Freedman, a study in defeat, sat in front of his locker.

● A study in defeat, Freedman sat in front of his locker.

○ Are your child and my child really being educated?

● Your child and my child. Are they really being educated?

Inversion. Inversion is the practice of rearranging elements within a sentence. For example, the sentence,

The giant liner eased into the narrow harbor.

can be inverted to read:

Into the narrow harbor eased the giant liner.

Inversion is an especially helpful device in effecting a smooth transition between sentences. Notice the paragraph below as it was originally cast. Then note the smooth blending achieved by the inversion of sentence elements.

○ The dog was weary and tired. He flopped heavily on the rug in front of the fire. He soon fell into a deep sleep. He was oblivious of the world about him.

● Weary and tired, the dog flopped heavily on the rug in front of the fire. Soon he fell into a deep sleep, oblivious of the world about him.

Logical arrangement. If a sentence is to attain maximum effectiveness, all detail must be arranged logically. Because logical arrangement can be understood best by examples, some representative deficiencies, followed by revisions, are given below.

○ The milers, quarter milers, half milers, and sprinters are scheduled to leave tomorrow for the national meet.

● The sprinters, quarter milers, half milers, and milers are scheduled to leave tomorrow for the national meet.

Note how the logical arrangement in the second sentence creates a pattern of association that makes the thought easier to grasp.

○ Invitations have been extended to juniors, sophomores, and seniors only.

● Invitations have been extended to sophomores, juniors, and seniors only.

Note the clarity achieved by the logical progression by class.

○ We saw sparrows, Siamese cats, Dalmatians, robins, alley cats, and Irish setters—all in the same yard.

● We saw sparrows and robins, Siamese cats and alley cats, Dalmatians and Irish setters—all in the same yard.

Note how the association of bird with bird, cat with cat, and dog with dog improves the sentence.

○ We shall be studying the French Revolution, World War II, and the rise of mercantilism.

● We shall be studying the rise of mercantilism, the French Revolution, and World War II.

Note how much easier it is to follow the sentence when the elements are arranged in chronological sequence.

Expanding sentences. As you revise your writing, you must know how to expand sentences properly. This practice, as the term implies, involves adding detail to a given sentence in order to improve that sentence, the whole paragraph, or the entire work.

For example, the bare sentence below may be expanded:

○ The plane eased down on the runway.

● The silver plane eased down on the long runway.

● The glistening silver plane eased down beautifully on the long, macadam runway.

One great problem you may have when you expand sentences is that of overloading the sentence. The following sentence, for instance, is badly overloaded:

○ The glistening, shimmering, silver plane eased down beautifully, perfectly, and impressively on the dull, black, macadam runway.

Deciding how much detail you use in a sentence as you expand it is, of course, subjective. You have to feel the rightness of the modifiers and the overall effect of the sentence—just as you must learn to feel a rightness to avoid overdressing for an informal party, overfurnishing a living room, or overplanting a garden. In short, you must rely on your sense of order and beauty.

Even after you feel reasonably certain that you have a sound critical judgment regarding overloaded sentences, you may find your judgment challenged. Critics have praised and disparaged the following sentence written by Thomas Wolfe in a letter to his mother. What do you think of it? In speaking of life, Wolfe says:

● It is savage, cruel, kind, noble, passionate, selfish, generous, stupid, ugly, beautiful, painful, joyous—it is all these, and more, and it's all these I want to know, and by God, I shall find, though they crucify me for it.   [May, 1923.]

Picture-making detail. When a writer composes a descriptive sentence, he must avoid the mistake of assuming that his words convey his full meaning when actually they fall far short of that goal. Quite often, the mistake arises because the writer completes the sentence in his mind; that is, he subconsciously adds to the bare sentence he has written the detail that he has either seen or imagined, but he does not pass the detail on to the reader. This sentence actually tells very little:

○ The child stood tugging at her mother's dress.

But by the addition of picture-making detail, the sentence can create a vivid scene:

● The chubby little girl, not more than three years old, kept tugging imploringly at her mother's dress as the two women stood exchanging bits of gossip.

Below are examples of bare sentences followed by sentences from well known writers. In each instance, the value of added picture-making detail is evident.

○ As Paul approached his house, he felt repelled by the whole scene.

● The nearer he approached the house, the more absolutely unequal Paul felt to the sight of it all; his ugly sleeping chamber;

the cold bath-room with the grimy zinc tub, the cracked mirror, the dripping spigots; his father, at the top of the stairs, his hairy legs sticking out from his night-shirt, his feet thrust into carpet slippers.   [Willa Cather, "Paul's Case," 1920.]

o   He is very fond of children, and he will do anything to please them.

●   Again, he is fond of children, a winning trait. He will throw himself into games with the little folk in the garden, make and mend their toys with great ingenuity, even read aloud from their books—and very droll it sounds in his thick-lipped pronunciation.   [Thomas Mann, "Disorder and Early Sorrow," 1936.]

o   It was a large house in a bad state of repair; while once residential, the street on which it was located had become part of the business district.

●   It was a big, squarish frame house that had once been white, decorated with cupolas and spires and scrolled balconies in the heavily lightsome style of the seventies, set on what had once been our most select street. But garages and cotton gins had encroached and obliterated even the august names of that neighborhood; only Miss Emily's house was left, lifting its stubborn and coquettish decay above the cotton wagons and gasoline pumps—an eyesore among eyesores.   [William Faulkner, "A Rose for Emily," 1950.]

o   Besides Claud, there was just one old man in the room.

●   The only man in the room besides Claud was a lean stringy fellow with a rusty hand spread out on each knee, whose eyes were closed as if he were asleep or dead or pretending to be so as not to get up and offer her his seat.   [Flannery O'Connor, "Revelation," 1964.]

Aphorisms. An *aphorism* is a concise statement of principle or sentiment. Aphorisms are used by famous essayists like Francis Bacon and Ralph Waldo Emerson, but lesser writers also use them. In fact, it is safe to say that the ability to develop a significant aphorism is one characteristic of an original thinker.

The danger in using aphorisms is the possibility of unconscious plagiarism. You will often write an aphorism only to realize later that you have actually taken it from a book or a lecture. Nonetheless, you must not relax your effort to write aphorisms. They can give power to all your writing and especially to your expository writing.

Below are some oft-quoted aphorisms. Where no source is credited, the aphorism is anonymous.

- Today is yesterday's tomorrow.

- The road to success is generally difficult to travel.

- The unexamined life is not worth living.   [Plato, "Apology."]

- The Religion that is afraid of science dishonors God and commits suicide.   [Ralph Waldo Emerson, *Journal*, 1831.]

- Reading maketh a full man; conference a ready man; and writing an exact man.   [Francis Bacon, "Of Studies."]

Below are some considerably less familiar aphorisms. Note, however, the manner in which each arrests the attention of the reader as it drives home its point.

- One's own time is always the obscurest epoch.   [Van Wyck Brooks, "The Silent Generation," 1938.]

- The practice of any art at any time is essentially a moral activity.   [Leslie Fiedler, "No, in Thunder!" 1960.]

- It is always an encouraging sign when people are rendered self-conscious and are forced to examine the basis of their ideals.   [Randolph Bourne, "This Older Generation," 1920.]

- Eternal vigilance is the price of life with most of the wild creatures.   [John Burroughs, "A Life of Fear," 1916.]

- Simple preference is a good and sufficient motive in determining one's choice of books, but it does not warrant a reader in conferring his impressions upon the world.   [Agnes Repplier, "Opinions," 1894.]

- Whatever the stars may say or whatever the sun's altitude may be, spring has not begun until the ice has melted and life begun to stir again.   [Joseph Wood Krutch, "April . . . the Day of the Peepers," 1961.]

- Yet new times call for new policies. Negro leadership, long attuned to agitation, must now perfect the art of organization.   [Martin Luther King, Jr., "Let Justice Roll Down," 1962.]

Below are instances of aphoristic writing in student papers.

- I learned early in my athletic career that the football player who relaxes is the football player who gets injured.

- The only sure way to beat most courses is to study, study, study.

- The person who buys an old second-hand car with high mileage is just buying a series of headaches.

- In his freshman year, the college student usually develops an important protection; he can tune out and screen out any lecturer.

- A gentleman's C is perfectly appropriate for a gentleman with a reserved place in his father's industry. But for the run-of-the-mill gentleman, a B strengthens his position by ten points and an A by twenty points.

- A hot day, a heavy lunch, and a dull lecture make a one o'clock class an ordeal.

Affirmation versus elements that subdue. Every sentence you write contains a certain degree of affirmation; that is, it conveys your message with a certain degree of authority. For instance,

Harrison is a liar.

is a very strong statement. It affirms its point resoundingly. On the other hand,

Harrison does not tell the truth.

conveys essentially the same idea but in more subdued tones.

Of course you must temper the degree of affirmation to achieve the effect you desire. Aside from choosing your words for shades of meaning (is the subject *mediocre, dull, stupid,* or *moronic,* for example) you must concern yourself most with employing positive or negative constructions as the situation may demand.

This sentence is a positive construction:

Lester is a poor writer.

Hence it is an affirmative assertion.

At the opposite pole is the negative construction:

Lester is not a good writer.

Hence it is a negative assertion. Generally speaking, the affirmative assertion is stronger than the negative.

A caution to be respected in handling negative assertions: unless handled carefully, the negative assertion may cloud meaning. For instance, the sentence,

○   I do not believe that Uncle Jim does not regard the President highly.

requires some untangling by the reader. However, the statements,

●   I do not believe that Uncle Jim holds the President in low regard.
●   I believe that Uncle Jim regards the President highly.

make their points much more clearly.

4.

Rhetorical devices

Although the word "rhetoric" has an elusive meaning, the expression "rhetorical devices" is often used by writers and teachers of writing to designate a variety of specific practices that improve expression.

The significance of the rhetorical device is quite evident. Many of the greatest speeches and writings of all time derive their power from rhetorical devices—battle cries, maxims, and ringing phrases, for example, have earned their creators lasting fame. Many rhetorical devices have meant the difference between acceptance and rejection of arguments crucial in the history of society.

Although rhetorical devices are commonly associated with important or great writing, they often appear in writing of a lesser nature. In fact, rhetorical devices are to be found in standard reports, memoranda, and similar routine writing.

The most significant rhetorical devices are listed and discussed in the following sections. Remember that your task is twofold: you must develop familiarity with the device itself, and you must learn how to incorporate it easily and naturally into your own writing. In each instance, therefore, think of the particular device as a resource upon which to draw as a particular situation may demand.

Analogy

The *analogy*—one of the most common and telling means of making a point—is a comparison of two situations with the intent of proving

33

that what is true for one is true for the other. For instance, the analogy of the human body to a machine has been used countless times. The thought behind the comparison is that each has a series of functions to perform, each requires proper care, and each must not be overtaxed. Hence we are cautioned, by comparison, to avoid strain, to obtain proper rest, and to respect the needs of the body accordingly—just as we must care properly for a machine.

Analogy crops up frequently in the Bible. The "man who walketh not in the counsel of the ungodly" is compared by analogy to a "tree planted by the rivers of water." Man is admonished to build his house of faith on rock rather than on sand; and lessons are taught by analogies to laborers in a vineyard and to travelers with lamps that require a certain oil.

The examples below are effective uses of analogies.

- It gives you a queer feeling if, late in life, you are ordered once again to write a school essay. But you obey automatically, like the old soldier who, at the word, "Attention," cannot help dropping whatever he may have in his hands and who finds his little fingers pressed along the seams of his trousers. [Sigmund Freud, "Some Reflections on Schoolboy Psychology."]

- The recent history of American education has paralleled that of American bread. By removing the hull of the wheat, bleaching to make the flour chalk-white, and by other chemical processes making the loaf soft enough for baby teeth and those of the aged, by chemical treatment to keep it damp within its wrapper, despite the pre-slicing which reduces the operations in the home kitchen—by elaborate treatment in the laboratory, American bread has been deprived of food values implicit in the old-fashioned stone-ground flour, and the yeast-raised, over-baked, brownish, granular, and hard-crusted loaf. To make up for the complex chemical destruction of vitamins, minerals, and other salubrious elements in our bread, the millers and bakers have injected all sorts of fortifying drugs and powders, until according to their avowals, the loaf is almost as good as if they hadn't tampered with it in the first place.   [Gordon Keith Chalmers, "Adjusting to Life," *The Republic and the Person*, 1952.]

● If you will take the longest street in New York, and travel up and down it, conning its features patiently until you know every house and window and lamppost and big and little sign by heart, and know them so accurately that you can instantly name the one you are abreast of when you are set down at random in that street in the middle of an inky black night, you will then have a tolerable notion of the amount and the exactness of a pilot's knowledge who carries the Mississippi River in his head. [Mark Twain, "The Gilded Age of Steamboating," 1873.]

● She reminded him of a juggler tossing knives; but the knives were blunt and she knew they would never cut her.   [Edith Wharton, "The Other Two," 1958.]

The following analogies are from student writing. How effective are they?

Answering that professor's questions is like jumping into a garbage vat. No matter what you do, you will emerge smelling bad.

Social life on this campus is one vast maze, with the student-rat always seeking a door to questionable success.

My early years were like a nonathletic person learning to ice skate—a series of pratfalls, bruises, and embarrassments.

Our last college president was like a wet noodle. He had no backbone; he was very hard to hold in one place; and he had a dubious final value.

Aside from making certain that an analogy you wish to use is sound and telling, you must be careful or your analogy may backfire. The writer, for example, who compares a dangerous civic condition to an infection that must be lanced may well be told that every infection should not be lanced; sometimes a milder course of action is in order. Similarly, the person who compares difficult periods in life to rainy days may well be told that rainy days are often eagerly anticipated.

Often, a weakness in an analogy can be demonstrated clearly, as in the passage below. David Dressler is arguing for certain reforms in criminal trial procedures. He has seized upon a weakness in an analogy advanced to defend an opposing viewpoint and, in the process, has strengthened his own argument.

● ... when I asked a Los Angeles police official whether police findings should not be shared with the defense, he replied, "Do the Dodgers give the Giants their signals?" No, but human beings are not baseballs, trials are not baseball games, and the stakes are not pennants. The liberty and perhaps the life of a defendant are at stake in every criminal trial. Police science should be employed in the interest of truth and justice, not to win a battle for one side.   [*Harper's*, July 1961]

Allusion

The terms "allusion" and "reference" are generally used synonymously, although some stylists prefer to make a fine distinction. They say the term "allusion" designates a reference to an original of widely known or lofty stature. For example, the following sentences reflect allusion in this sense:

If Frank was a genius in that class, he was certainly hiding his *light under a bushel.*   [*Sermon on the Mount.*]

Let's not look for any *daggers in the air.*   [Shakespeare, *Macbeth.*]

Like Roland, he was forced to *blow the horn.*   [*The Saga of Roland.*]

The term *reference*, on the other hand, designates a reference to a more prosaic original. For instance, the statement that an oft-married man is a "Bluebeard" is considered reference.

When attempting to prove a point by reference, select one that is immediately meaningful and likely to remain so. When James Thurber, for instance, says in *University Days* that his botany professor was "beginning to quiver all over, like Lionel Barrymore," he incurs the risk of losing effectiveness with the passing of time, of becoming dated. For readers old enough to remember Barrymore, the reference has both force and humor. For others, it has almost no impact.

The danger of becoming dated has been avoided by Gordon W. Allport in the following sentence:

- A very few Shakespeares, Lincolns, or Ghandis could put the world immeasurably ahead in its search for wisdom and for peace.   ["Uniqueness in Students," 1960.]

Antithesis

Antithesis is the device of presenting two or more extremes in practices or concepts to emphasize or accentuate a main idea through contrast, capitalizing on the impact gained by placing opposites side by side. A common example is a sentence of this kind:

We are interested in success, not failure; in strength, not weakness; in action, not inertia.

Examine these instances of antithesis taken from the works of well known writers:

- Ideally, good conversation has the smoothness and the brilliance of Davis Cup tennis; in reality, as we all know, it is a mass of stumbles, clumsy returns, and points missed.   [Jacques Barzun, "The Care and Feeding of the Mind," 1959.]

- She preferred rudeness to kindness, insult to compliment, discourtesy to graciousness. Claire loved hate and hated love. [Lester Babb, "Claire," 1957.]

- It was the best of times, it was the worst of times, it was the age of wisdom, it was the age of foolishness, it was the epoch of belief, it was the epoch of incredulity, it was the season of

Light, it was the season of Darkness, it was the spring of hope, it was the winter of despair, we had everything before us, we had nothing before us, we were all going direct to Heaven, we were all going direct the other way—in short, the period was so far like the present period, that some of its noisiest authorities insisted on its being received, for good or for evil, in the superlative degree of comparison only.

There were a king with a large jaw and a queen with a plain face, on the throne of England; there were a king with a large jaw and a queen with a fair face, on the throne of France. In both countries it was clearer than crystal to the lords of the State preserves of loaves and fishes, that things in general were settled for ever.   [Charles Dickens, *A Tale of Two Cities*, 1859.]

Below are instances of antithesis taken from student themes.

American history was both my most exhilarating and my most depressing course. It was exhilarating because of the very interesting lectures and readings. It was depressing because we never had any class discussions.

Al Porter, brilliant academically but stupid socially, was dating Beth Fox, a chatterbox with her friends but a sphinx with strangers.

Dinner conversation with my aunt and uncle is unpredictable and predictable. Unpredictable because you never know what "friend" they will pan. Predictable because you can be sure they will keep at it all evening.

Paradox

A *paradox* is a statement that appears to contradict itself but which, by virtue of the apparent contradiction, makes a forceful statement.

For instance, the statements,

The only thing that is permanent is change.

and

The cheapest way to patch a roof is the most expensive way to patch a roof.

are paradoxes.

Each of those statements opens up a large area of thought.

Paradoxical situations are common, and so paradoxical statements are numerous. Historians speak of "looking ahead by looking back"; philosophers speak of "learning about happiness by learning about sadness"; and educators speak of "learning by unlearning." In each instance, a paradoxical statement results from an examination of a condition that has proved to be paradoxical.

Balance

Balance, which is quite similar to parallelism, is the practice of pairing elements in such a manner that the reader senses a level, or balanced, quality in the writing. To illustrate, the sentence below is not balanced.

o   Doc is a strong swimmer, a golfer, and a top flight tennis player.

It can be balanced quite easily:

●   Doc is a strong swimmer, a good golfer, and a top flight tennis player.

The following examples of balanced writing have been extracted from well known writings.

●   To every thing there is a season, and a time to every purpose under the heaven;
A time to be born, and a time to die; a time to plant, and a time to pluck up that which is planted;

A time to kill, and a time to heal; a time to break down, and a
time to build up;
A time to weep, and a time to laugh; a time to mourn, and a
time to dance . . .   [Eccles. 3.]

● It is the fate of those who toil at the lower employments of life
to be rather driven by the fear of evil, than attracted by the
prospect of good; to be exposed to censure, without hope of
praise; to be disgraced by miscarriage, or punished for neglect,
where success would have been without applause, and diligence
without reward.   [Samuel Johnson, Preface to the *Dictionary*,
1755.]

● There is a time in every man's education when he arrives at the
conviction that envy is ignorance; that imitation is suicide; that
he must take himself for better for worse as his portion; that
though the wide universe is full of good, no kernel of nourishing
corn can come to him but through his toil bestowed on that
plot of ground which is given to him to till.   [Ralph Waldo
Emerson, "Self-Reliance," 1840.]

The following examples of balanced writing have been extracted
from student writings.

My roommate was constantly torn between opposing forces—
study or fail, mother or girl friend, French horn or piccolo,
sundaes or starvation diet.

The dean of men is a study in vacillation, a straw on the
academic sea, an authority on the subject of sharing bathrooms
in peace and tranquility.

His lectures were dull and his speech was horrendous; his ties
were nightmarish and his suits were ghastly; his stories were bad
and his humor was insufferable. Yet somehow he managed to
impart a great amount of helpful material, a large corpus of
valuable insights.

The leave taking was brief and formal, yet sad and enervating.

The new dorm counselor is a bright light academically but a dull bulb socially. He is also wearisome in his monologues and an apparition in his pajamas.

Repetition

Repetition—the practice of repeating for emphasis—is an especially difficult device to control. In the hands of a capable writer, it can achieve a powerful effect. In the hands of lesser writers, it often falls flat. The most important aspect of handling repetition, therefore, is recognizing when you have used it capably.

Below are some relatively successful instances from student writing:

> Slowly, slowly, the dean thumbed through the cards to see if the Executive Committee had approved my readmission.

> My father always thinks of the right answer too late—too late to be of any real help.

Below is a passage by Joseph Conrad, one of the most successful users of repetition. As you read this passage, you must realize that Conrad possesses a most unusual ability to hover perilously close to the brink of overuse of repetition without quite falling. He is somewhat like the stunt flyer: he executes feats that less skillful flyers must not attempt.

● I need not tell you what it is to be knocking about in an open boat. I remember nights and days of calm, when we pulled, we pulled, and the boat seemed to stand still, as if bewitched within the circle of the sea horizon. I remember the heat, the deluge of rain-squalls that kept us bailing for dear life (but filled our water-cask), and I remember sixteen hours on end with a mouth dry as a cinder and a steering-oar over the stern to keep my first command head on to a breaking sea. I did not know how good a man I was till then. I remember the drawn faces, the dejected figures of my two men, and I remember my youth and the feeling that will never come back any more—the feeling that I could last for ever, outlast the sea, the earth, and all men; the deceitful feeling that lures us on to joys, to perils, to love, to vain effort—to death; the triumphant conviction of strength, the heat of life in the handful of dust, the glow in the heart that with every year grows dim, grows cold, grows small, and expires—and expires, too soon, too soon—before life itself. [Joseph Conrad, *Youth*, 1902.]

Restatement

Restatement is a variation of repetition. It is the practice of expressing the same thought more than once using synonymous terms. The purpose, of course, is to make the thought more emphatic.

Below are examples that show how these uses of restatement may vary from the obvious to the subtle.

● We must think of our children, the very young of today who will be the decision makers of tomorrow. [Atlanta *Constitution*, June 14, 1972.]

● The great factor in history is the fallibility of man. The one thing we can count on in life is that people will blunder. [Edward Sandford Martin, "Our Convalescent World," 1927.]

● Authority is not to give in; it is to remain firm in its commitment to preserve the essential asymmetry and the indelible generational separation, even if this means being seen as a "square" or "straight arrow." [Thomas J. Cottle, "Parent and Child—The Hazards of Equality," 1969.]

● By making education the slave of scholarship, the university . . . has disowned what teaching has always meant: a care and concern for the future of man, a Platonic love of the species, not for what it is but for what it might be. [William Arrowsmith, "The Heart of Education: Turbulent Teachers," 1967.]

The greatest problem in handling restatement is, once again, that of keeping the device in bounds. If you are not careful, you may well sound foolish or redundant.

The following are instances of questionable or poor use of restatement.

○ This question is serious; it is important; it is significant.

○ Every undergraduate student in this college—every freshman, every sophomore, every junior, and every senior—must accept his responsibility.

○ We must canvas every house in our township—on every highway and every byway, on every street and every road, on every avenue and every boulevard—we must canvas them all.

Foreign phrases

On some occasions, a word or expression from a foreign language creates a note of "justrightness." This is especially true when English lacks a really precise equivalent—as in the instance of the French *cuisine* or the Italian *paisano*—and when a foreign expression is rich in traditional appeal; for example, the German *sturm und drang* and the Latin *caveat emptor*.

However, you must guard against the possibility of being supercilious or artificial—as were the graduates of finishing schools of another time who mastered eight or ten French expressions and then used them ostentatiously.

Below are some rather effective uses of foreign words and expressions.

● If such views are held about art, it follows *a fortiori* whoever holds them must hold similar views about criticism.   [T. S. Eliot, "The Function of Criticism," 1932.]

● For such a temper, Adams was not the best companion, since his own gaiety was not *folle* . . .   [Henry Adams, "The Dynamo and the Virgin," 1931.]

- By knowing modern nations, I mean not merely knowing their *belles lettres*, but knowing also what has been done by such men as Copernicus, Galileo, Newton, Darwin.   [Matthew Arnold, "Literature and Science," 1882.]

- I suppose the *prima-facie* view which the public at large would take of a university, considered as a place of education, is nothing more or less than a place for acquiring a great deal of knowledge on a great many subjects.   [John Henry Newman, "Knowledge Viewed in Relation to Learning," 1873.]

- I like to see my old friends—whom distance cannot diminish—figuring up in the air (so they appear to our optics), yet on *terra firma* still . . .   [Charles Lamb, "Old China," 1833.]

Direct quotation

A writer sometimes can best make his point by using a direct quotation. In portraying a reaction of children, for instance, you frequently cannot improve upon the effect obtained by reproducing the exact quotation—including the mispronunciations, grammatical errors, and distorted structures. Similarly, you can often capture an element of personality with a direct quotation.

Note the examples below, all of which are taken from student writing.

Old Mrs. Harnish expressed one of her "Dear, dear, dear" reactions.

As usual, Grandfather was "agin the whole dang business."

Three-year-old Horace Lattimore Brittingham III suddenly "frowed" his father's fedora into the punch bowl, causing something of excitement among the guests.

The direct quotation can also be used to cast a special light on a complex or a multifaceted question. In this instance, it serves to create a range of viewpoints by presenting an opinion other than the writer's. Russell Lynes, for example, in his book *The Tastemakers* has a section entitled, "Highbrow, Lowbrow, Middlebrow," in which he defines these three terms. To define "highbrow," he employs with an appealing sense of humor three direct quotations on the subject.

● The highbrows come first. Edgar Wallace, who was certainly not a highbrow himself, was asked by a newspaper reporter in Hollywood some years ago to define one. "What is a highbrow?" he said. "A highbrow is a man who has found something more interesting than women."

　　Presumably at some time in every man's life there are things he finds more interesting than women: alcohol, for example, or the World Series. Mr. Wallace has only partially defined the highbrow. Brander Matthews came closer when he said that "a highbrow is a person educated beyond his intelligence," and A. P. Herbert came closest of all when he wrote that "a highbrow is the kind of person who looks at a sausage and thinks of Picasso."

Novelists, of course, rely heavily on the device of direct quotation. Thomas Hardy changes spellings of conventional words to reproduce the accents and hence the authenticity of Egdon Heath. Ernest Hemingway frequently presents the main action of his story ("The Killers," for one) through the direct quotation of unconventional language.

One of the most frequently cited and most potent uses of the direct quotation is the one on which the high point of Mark Twain's best novel, *Huckleberry Finn*, turns. Huck, with his great adventure now behind him, stands frightened at the prospect of life within the staid and convention-ridden society to which he must return—a society that is certain to restrict the freedom he prizes so highly. He announces his decision on the matter in what is considered one of the great quotations in American literature:

● But I reckon I got to light out for the territory ahead of the rest, because Aunt Sally she's going to adopt me and sivilize me, and I can't stand it. I been there before.   [1885.]

Understatement

Understatement, often associated with British humor, is especially effective as a device for obtaining a humorous or sarcastic tone. The examples below are from well known writers.

- I fear I cannot picture America as altogether an Elysium. [Oscar Wilde, "Stranger in America," 1905.]
- It is possible to get an education at a university. It has been done . . .   [Lincoln Steffens, *Autobiography*, 1936.]
- We were in no danger—the wind was blowing the vapor to the north-northwest of us—but the feeling seemed to take hold that this wasn't necessarily the Prophet Isaiah's day.   [Daniel Lang, *An Inquiry Into Enoughness*, 1965.]

The following examples from college writing are also effective.

Pete, with his scuffed shoes and off-beat attire, did not attract much attention as a candidate for the role of "best dressed man."

My mathematics instructor is something less than the soul of effervescence.

His table manners contribute precious little to the atmosphere necessary for an "adventure in good eating."

When our plane was landing at the airport, it skidded off the runway, struck a parked gasoline truck, and ripped off a wing. Somehow, I don't like to see wings ripped off planes in which I am riding.

Unexpected turn

To achieve a startling or a humorous effect, the writer often employs the device of the unexpected turn. He presents a thought that is startling because of its incongruity, its seeming inappropriateness, or its general atmosphere of unexpectedness. Some representative instances follow.

- Men will confess to treason, murder, arson, false teeth, or a wig. How many of them will own up to a lack of humor?   [Frank Moore Colby, "The Pursuit of Humor," 1962.]

- It is a mistake for a sculptor or a painter to speak or write very often about his job. It releases tension needed for his work. [Henry Moore, "Notes on Sculpture," 1969.]

- Yes, working one's way through college has its values. It is better than not going to college. It is also better than playing one's way through college. But it is not better than studying one's way through college.   [Ralph Cooper Hutchinson, "Work Your Way through College?" 1940.]

- Today we ask only one thing of our athletic heroes and heroines: the impossible. That's all. We merely ask them to be generous, to be sweet, attractive, sensitive citizens of the world. And at the same time to be winners.   [John R. Tunis, "What They Call Sportsmanship," 1941.]

- Thoreau said he required of every writer, first and last, a simple and sincere account of his own life. Having delivered himself of this chesty dictum, he proceeded to ignore it. In his books and even in his enormous journal, he withheld or disguised most of the facts from which an understanding of his life could be drawn.   [E. B. White, "A Slight Sound at Evening," 1962.]

- There is only one thing more foolish than going to hear a lecture and that, of course, is giving a lecture.   [J. B. Priestly, "Lectures," 1955.]

The following examples of the unexpected turn are from student writing.

When my father writes checks for my college expenses, he is careful, thoughtful, professional, and stingy.

The examinations for that course are invariably challenging, all-inclusive, and devastating.

The professor's attire was a constant source of wonder to us; we always wondered whether he had got it from the Salvation Army or the Goodwill deposit box.

The carefully dressed man at the next table was eating like a bird—a mountain eagle.

The football team was composed of perfect gentlemen—when judged by Stone Age standards.

As a cook, my Aunt Jane is a marvel. She can broil a sirloin in such a way that it tastes like reclaimed rubber.

Last year my roommate achieved a remarkable record. In addition to a straight A average, he managed to be in five taprooms when they were raided.

Intensifiers

An *intensifier* is a word invoked to make a statement stronger. Although the intensifier is viewed grammatically as a modifier, its purpose is actually to make the meaning more emphatic—hence more intense. The italicized words and expressions below are intensifiers.

I *honestly* don't think the job is well done.

Certainly the President must know his assistant's weaknesses.

He is *indeed* a competent performer.

Thiessen is a *really* reliable officer.

The chairman is, *to be sure*, right in his ruling.

The following sentences illustrate the use of intensifiers (italicized) in the writing of well known authors.

● I had already—I had *indeed* instantly—seen that he was a delightful creature. [Henry James, "The Author of Beltraffio," 1885.]

- *As a matter of fact*, our great-grandfathers, who never went anywhere, *in actuality* had more experience of the world than we have, who have seen everything.   [D. H. Lawrence, *Phoenix*, 1936.]

- Let us, *I say*, be agreed about the meaning of the terms we are using.   [Matthew Arnold, "Literature and Science," 1885.]

- This, *thank goodness*, is the first warm and balmy night of the year: the first frogs are singing.   [Eric Sevareid, "The Dark of the Moon," 1958.]

Figures of speech

The term "figure of speech" becomes clear with an understanding of the terms "literal" and "figurative."

Literal means "according to the letter." When a pilot is flying a plane, he is, literally speaking, "up in the clouds."

Figurative means "a poetic or nonliteral use of language." When this same pilot, upon returning home, learns that he has won $10,000 in a lottery, he may express his joy by stating that he is "up in the clouds." Now, of course, he is speaking figuratively; that is, he is using a figure of speech.

The role of figurative language in our daily lives is demonstrated by a rather surprising fact. In ordinary conversation, one rarely speaks for as long as one minute (literally speaking) without using a figure of speech. We would be lost without such figures of speech as "down in the dumps," "in the red," "ahead of the pack," "behind the eight ball," and numerous others.

The significance of figures of speech for you, the writer, is evident. The final quality of much writing is in direct proportion to the power of the figures used.

The eight most common figures of speech are discussed below.

Metaphor is an implied comparison of two unlike objects that have one point in common. To illustrate: in the sentence,

The bleeding prize fighter became a savage animal.

the two unlike objects are, of course, the prize fighter and the animal.

Simile is a comparison of two unlike objects that is accomplished by using "as" or "like." To illustrate:

The bleeding prize fighter was like a wounded animal.

Personification is the attribution of animate qualities or abilities to inanimate objects. For example:

The books were *shouting* to be read.

Alliteration is the repetition of a letter or a sound for the purpose of emphasis. For example:

Peterson's *p*each *p*ies *p*rovide a *p*leasing *p*arty *p*astry.

Hyperbole is exaggeration that is not meant to deceive. For example:

He had a bump over his eye as *big as a watermelon.*

Metonymy is the practice of using the name of an object for that of another object or concept to which it bears a logical relationship. For example, "crown" is used for "right to rule" in the following sentence:

George VI was given the *crown* when Edward abdicated.

Synecdoche, which is closely related to metonymy, is the use of the part for the whole or the whole for the part. For example:

Give us this day our daily *bread*.

The President of the United States awaited *Russia's* answer.

Litotes is understatement, usually expressed in negative terms, employed for emphasis. For example:

Shakespeare was not a bad writer.

Below are some figures of speech taken from the writings of well known authors.

- When the glacier came down out of the north, *crunching* hills and *gouging* valleys, some *adventuring* rampart of the ice *climbed* the Baraboo Hills and fell back into the outlet gorge of the Wisconsin River. [Aldo Leopold, "Marshland Elegy," 1949.]

- On the twenty-ninth of July, in 1943, my father died . . . On the morning of August third we drove him to the graveyard through a *wilderness of smashed plate glass.* [James Baldwin, *Notes of a Native Son*, 1955.]

- But to enjoy freedom . . . we have to control ourselves. We must not squander our powers, helplessly and ignorantly, *squirting half the house in order to water a single rose-bush* . . . [Virginia Woolf, "How Should One Read a Book," 1932.]

- Every time he shut his eyes, trying to sleep, Mr. Thompson's mind *started up* and *began to run like a rabbit.* It *jumped* from one thing to another, trying to *pick up a trail* here or there that would straighten out what had happened that day he killed Mr. Hatch. [Katherine Anne Porter, "Noon Wine," 1939.]

- Thus the young American grows up to see life as a *cornucopia spilling its plenty* into the lap of those who are there to take it. [Max Lerner, "Growing Up in America," 1957.]

- In Dallas, still booming while much of the country endures a recession, the family-controlled *Morning News* and the Times Mirror Company's *Times Herald* are *locked in a shoot-out* for dominance of one of *metropolitan journalism's* few *remaining frontiers.* [Dennis Holder, *Washington Journalism Review*, April 1982.]

5.

Humor, mild satire, and parody

Humor and satire are among the most important stylistic devices in the entire realm of writing. They can achieve results obtainable in no other way—as proven by the many satirical writings and humorous selections that have survived beyond their own time.

Humor

It is not easy to handle humor successfully. Writing humorously is often made challenging by the fact that much humor can have, at best, a limited appeal. That which is hilariously funny to one person is often stupidly dull to a second; and that which is very pleasing to one audience is lifeless or trite to another. Therefore, you may have a real problem in finding humorous elements that have widespread attraction.

Nonetheless, you must not be discouraged. Most people have acquired a store of knowledge and experience that contains elements that can produce appealing humor—even though it may be of a limited sort. Your task is to discover those elements and then capitalize properly upon them.

Examine these passages from writers who use humor with clear success.

- If I had the misfortune to be a college president again, then, I hope I would retain enough faith in the human intellect to listen carefully to the faculty, the students, the janitorial staff, the trustees, and even the unspeakably corrupt Townies who surround our righteous communities. [Stringfellow Barr, *The Center Magazine*, May 1969.]

- My uncle Henry, unable to go out for ducks in summer, kept his eagle eye in trim by shooting such chickens as were needed for the table. He would go down to the barnyard on Sunday morning, draw a bead upon a strutting cockerel, and lift off its head with the ease of a laryngologist fetching an adenoid. [H. L. Mencken, *The Days of H. L. Mencken*, 1947.]

- On any class day in winter you can enter [the Harvard class building erected in honor of Ralph Waldo Emerson] and see Frank Duveneck's statue of him buried under the coats and hats. Somehow, this symbolizes what has happened to Emerson. [Howard Mumford Jones, "The Iron String," 1950.]

- It takes a politician to run a government. A statesman is a politician who's been dead maybe ten or fifteen years. [Harry S. Truman, 1950.]

- Miami residents don't wear many clothes, but they have more to hide, per capita, than inhabitants of any other city in the nation. They plot secret military missions in Cuba and carry out secret commercial missions in Colombia. At dockside bars, exiles from corrupt regimes and other political intriguers mingle with smugglers and conventional criminals. [John Rothchild, *Harper's*, May 1982.]

Below are some humorous lines from student writing.

The college bookstore is the most democratic place on campus; everybody gets the same rude treatment.

In our home town, all the old, retired men congregate in the town square where they seem half asleep until a short skirt passes. Then they man their battle stations.

My blind date had the appeal of a pan of cold mashed potatoes.

I've been in dozens of Sears, Roebuck stores, and they all smell uniformly alike—oily peanuts, mustard on hot dogs, cheap clothing, and stale fertilizer.

The telephone company isn't a monopoly. It just doesn't have any competitors because it chokes them to death as soon as they show any real signs of life.

When my philosophy professor is particularly pleased with an answer, he does a little dance step that falls midway between a rhumba and a waltz.

Mild satire

Mild satire—which is really a blend of sarcasm and humor—is one of the common techniques of popular critical writing. It is found in newspaper reviews, magazine articles, political tracts, and advertising. Anytime that a writer passes a pleasant but mildly caustic judgment upon something that annoys him, he is using mild satire.

Since mild satire can take many forms, the definition given above is, of necessity, quite broad. Mild satire is so close to other forms of humor and may make use of such a wide variety of devices, including sarcasm and the quick turn of phrase, that isolating it for precise definition is impossible. Yet you can recognize mild satire easily after meeting it a few times. More important, you can learn quickly to use this device appropriately and effectively.

Below are representative illustrations.

- Schlesinger is an Englishman: like many of his countrymen who come here to make films, he sees all America as one huge annex to Disneyland.   [Stephen Farber, "End of the Road," 1970.]

- Dr. Dooley . . . treats professional, college, high school and even grade school athletes. The majority come from the Los Angeles area, but not a few from other parts of the country, Dooley perhaps being better known among participants than physicians.   [Bil Gilber, "Athletes in a Turned-On World," 1969.]

- Thomas O. Paine had reportedly ... back in 1968, after the success of Apollo 8 ... called the flight "a triumph of the squares—meaning the guys with crew cuts and slide rules who read the Bible and get things done."

  ... I had thought that circling the moon was a victory for everybody; millions of people who might not consider themselves square certainly had helped finance it. And if the squares were the victors, who were the losers?   [George B. Leonard, "A Place for Snakes as well as Naked Lovers," 1970.]

- Genius is not an exclusive possession of the righteous, nor is an artist obliged to edify the local chamber of commerce. [James F. Scott, "Beat Literature and the American Teen Cult," 1962.]

- Somewhere in the history of our Republic there may have been a high government official who said he had been treated fairly by the press, but for the life of me, however, I can't think of one.   [Walter Cronkite, "What It's Like to Broadcast News," 1970.]

Here are some random selections from student writings.

The real estate salesman said it was a lovely location, Yes, it was a lovely location for swamp flies, mosquitoes, insectivorous birds, and pet alligators.

My neighbor has telescopic vision when he watches the activities around our home.

Her economics professor was a gentleman in every way necessary for success as a slave driver.

Old Mr. Planter and his wife deserve each other. They are undeviatingly tightfisted, mean, and suspicious.

When the boss took his first plane ride, he thought the thing was taking him to Heaven. He should know better. That's no place for him.

The irate police officer whistled down the car, approached the chastened driver, and, his face bristling with rage, whispered sweet nothings in a soft, well modulated voice.

Parody

Parody is a variation of a well known original for the purpose of gaining a strong or humorous impact. If, for example, you were to say to a person trying to learn to cook, "If at first you don't succeed, fry, fry again!" you would be using parody.

Although the general public most often encounters parody in political writing and advertisements, the parody is also used in many other types of writing.

- Speaking disparagingly of television programs, Richard E. Peck says, "Every week *The Fugitive* escapes being executed by an unjust society, and his audience stays with him through thin and thin."   ["Films, Television, and Tennis," 1970.]

- ... when people like Health Commissioner Edward O'Rourke start transposing 368 rate bites into a total of 8 million New York rats, one feels a strong impulse to take arms against the rising sea of instant statistics.   [Ezra Bowen, "New York by the Numbers," 1969.]

- [Speaking disparagingly of trans-Atlantic air travel, L. E. Sissman says,] There is a big bus line in the sky, dedicated to the proposition that Americans will put up good money (or good credit) to be conveyed in maximum discomfort reminiscent of cross-country bus travel in the thirties or day-coach travel during World War II, to distant places. Nor does their ordeal end when they arrive at the promised (but not delivered) land. The first-class or deluxe hotels are carpeted with the serried BOAC bags of fellow travelers; the white and naked beaches of the tour brochures are discovered to be as populous as Coney Island; the gorgeous tombs and ruins swarm with ant colonies of unquiet Americans ...   [*The Atlantic*, September 1971.]

- Every morning when Mayor John Lindsay arises, he looks into his mirror and asks, "Mirror, mirror, on the wall, who's the fairest mayor of all?" and the mirror answers, "You are, of course."   [William F. Buckley, newspaper column, May 13, 1970.]

Here are some anonymous parodies.

His motto is "Don't put off until tomorrow what you can do the day after."

To cheat or not to cheat, that is the question.

He is a wolf in wolf's clothing.

You could have knocked me over with a steam roller!

That hockey player believes in "glove your enemy."

6.

Undesirable conditions in expression

In addition to the useful stylistic devices presented in the preceding chapter, you must be aware of certain pitfalls or traps into which the unsuspecting writer can easily fall. A discussion of the most common follows.

Jargon

To understand the dangers of using jargon, you must first know its two principal definitions. According to the first definition, jargon is, broadly speaking, *inexact* or almost meaningless *language* that characterizes the usage of a group of trade, business, or professional people. In this sense, it frequently reflects a tone of pomposity or aloofness. This, in turn, creates a suspicion that the user may be enveloping a simple matter in an atmosphere of complexity or erudition.

When educationists, for example, speak of "language laboratory writing experiences" (writing compositions in class), "teaching in terms of the inherent basic personality factors in the immediate situation" (teaching in terms of the student's personality), and "genuinely realized and deeply experienced felt needs" (the material the child feels he will need), they can be accused of using jargon.

The most serious objections to this kind of jargon are those cited above: the listener or reader may doubt the user's intellectual honesty and the language is frequently vague or inexact.

The second definition of jargon is, "the special language of knowledgeable people in a given field." For instance, sports writers often use such terms as "ump," "glove" the ball, "fireman" (relief pitcher), "club" (team), "mentor" (coach), "fan" (strike out) the batter, "position" the players on the field.

For you, as a writer, this second type of jargon can be very important. Often you will be forced to use it in the interest of precise speech.

For instance, there are no acceptable synonyms for the following examples of jargon: "kill" a story, "squeegee" a window, "birdie" a hole, "soup up" a car, silence a "kibitzer," "red dog" the offense, "emcee" a cafe show. Therefore, when the circumstances demand, you must be prepared to use language such as this.

Study the following examples of jargon.

- *Avatar* was the last of the original papers to suspend publication; the others moved further into sexploitation and acquired a new audience.   [Jesse Kornbluth, "The Underground and How It Went," 1969.]

The use of "sexploitation" in this sentence is expressive and attractive.

- Ordinarily, though, much of the work is done almost in bankerish fashion from Saigon . . .   [Michael J. Arlen, "Television and the Press in Viet Nam," 1967.]

"Bankerish" means remaining aloof from the action. Can you find a better way to say what is meant?

Purple prose

Purple prose designates expression that is seriously exaggerated in its modifiers, detail, and general phraseology—all in an attempt to be poetic or grandiloquent.

You must avoid purple prose for one great reason: you run the risk of losing any chance to be convincing. The writer who uses purple prose is like the young man who wears garish clothing to a sedate gathering: He cannot hope to impress.

Below is a paragraph filled with purple prose.

○   The downy-soft blanket of new fallen snow covered the soft earth tenderly and beautifully. The majestic trees, like denizens of the forest, stood silently and eloquently reaching heavenward toward the deep gray sky. Here and there, a forlorn bird hopped and twittered to make an eerie music to accompany the lovely and unusual scene.

Trite expressions

If you are to write effectively, you must avoid the trite expression—also termed the "cliche" or the "bromide." A trite expression is one that has been so overworked that it has little impact.

Such trite expressions as "quick as lightning," "sly as a fox," "quick as a deer," "razor sharp," and "smooth as silk" condemn the writer for lack of originality—or worse still, for falling into patterns of meaningless expression.

Platitudes

A *platitude* is a supposedly profound statement that is actually either self-evident or almost universally familiar. Generally, the platitude is phrased in a pompous or overbearing manner.

The following are platitudes:

○   Our generation, like the generations before it, will go down in the golden pages of history.

○   Tomorrow the sun will rise, and we shall all go about our daily business.

○   As it must to all men, death came yesterday to Mr. Albert J. Prentice.

○   The laborer lifts his strong hands in a daily effort to earn his bread by the sweat of his brow.

○   And I warn every man, woman, and child within the sound of my voice that the world will eventually come to an end.

The dangers inherent in the use of the platitude are rather easy to discern. The user appears to be shallow and artificial.

Euphemisms

A euphemism is a word or expression used to replace one more harsh or offensive to the sensitivities. For example, "washroom" and "powder room" are euphemisms for "toilet."

No final, all-inclusive statement can be made regarding the use of euphemisms. They are shunned, for instance, in the world of journalism, but they are used heavily in the publications of religious groups. Hence you must be prepared to employ euphemisms as the situation may require. A sympathy note to a friend whose father has just died prematurely may demand such euphemisms as "passed away" and "untimely loss" rather than "died" and "sudden death." Similarly, euphemisms are needed in conveying distressing information. The college student who is expelled because of failing grades should not be told, "You are hereby informed that you have failed out of this college." Instead, he should be advised, "We are sorry to inform you that because of your unsatisfactory grade average, we are compelled by official regulations to remove you from the rolls."

Overstatement

Overstatement is a device generally to be avoided because it detracts from precise expression. When a writer states,

○   This is the best solution possible.

he is on questionable ground because of the extent of the claim. The demanding reader often considers the writer of such a statement to be a loose or careless thinker.

Some claim can be made, of course, for the use of overstatement. In fact, one of the most famous of twentieth century figures, Winston Churchill, was given to overstatement, as in the well-known quotation from his address to the House of Commons on August 20, 1940:

- Never in the field of human conflict was so much owed by so many to so few.

Also, overstatement is the essence of much day-to-day expression, as in

- When she gets the news, she will rip you from limb to limb.

Despite any argument in favor of overstatement, the fact remains that it detracts from precision of expression because the listener or the reader must invoke some qualification. When a person hears or reads,

○ Harbison is a perfect shortstop.

he immediately has to scale down the statement to realize that Harbison is an excellent, but not a perfect, shortstop. Mortal man cannot be perfect.

Temporary suspension

The term *temporary suspension* is used to denote interruptions of thought within a sentence as well as interruptions of thought within such longer units as paragraphs and chapters. Note how the verb phrase is interrupted in the sentence, o   We remembered that we *had*, after we had eaten our lunch of meat, potatoes, and peas, *forgotten* to order any fruit juice.

Note how the description of the teakwood is interrupted in the paragraph below:

o   As the tide receded, a large beam of teakwood was visible on the beach. The sun was casting beautiful shades of many colors across the slowly moving water, and latestayers were bundling under sweaters and blankets as the air grew slightly chilly. In scattered spots, a lone bather was jumping up in the water and then diving into the large waves. Evidently the teakwood was from the deck of an old aircraft carrier.

Although you may occasionally interrupt a thought without serious loss, you must be on guard against any use of temporary suspension lest your readers lose their way.

Ephemeral words and phrases

At any given time, there are in general use words and phrases that have sprung suddenly from known or unknown sources, that will enjoy the short life of a fashion or fad, and then will fade into oblivion with little possibility of being revived.

Frequently the nonspecialist in language designates these usages as "slang," but more properly they should be termed "ephemeral language."* Although this language is sometimes invention or corruption ("brunch," "geezer," "wifty"), it is often composed of conventional words that have been assigned new meanings ("cool," "groovy," "swift").

You must beware ephemeral language because (1) the word or phrase may be too broad to have any precise meaning and (2) the

*Actually, the term "slang" is so broad and inexact that most specialists in language neither use the term nor attempt to define it.

word or phrase, because it is soon forgotten, may quickly cause your writing to sound silly or dated. For example, the word "square" ("conventional," "conservative") is really too broad to contribute any degree of preciseness to a sentence and, in a relatively short time, will probably be thoroughly passé.

To appreciate the cautions cited above, you need only examine sentences such as the following:

○   Jimmy wants to see you—but fast. ("But" is used as an intensifier. c. 1945)

○   The double bubble gave the audience a large charge. (The very attractive girl pleased the audience greatly. c. 1948)

○   It's going to be a great party. I'm sure we'll have a giant time. (c. 1950)

○   My, how sanitary! (Expression of approval. c. 1951)

○   The course wasn't hard hard. It was just hard. (The doubling of the modifier indicates a degree of emphasis. c. 1959)

○   See you later, alligator. After a while, crocodile. (Expressions of leave-taking. "Alligator" and "crocodile" mean, loosely, "friend." c. 1961)

○   The book is about yea long. ("Yea" means "that." The sentence is accompanied by an indication of length made with the hands. c. 1962)

○   Let's split for the lunch bit. ("Split" means "leave." "Bit" means "something to be done"—as *study bit, vacation bit, exam bit*. c.1963)

○   She wasn't about to leave. ("About to" means "had no intention of." c. 1965)

○   Chemistry isn't my bag. ("Bag" means an area of competence or interest. c. 1970)

○   The bartender was making off-the-wall remarks. ("Off-the-wall" means "indecent," "obscene," "gauche," "offensively inappropriate." c. 1982)

7.

The nature of the paragraph

The paragraph, like the sentence, is a fundamental challenge to the writer's skill. To be successful, the writer must be able (1) to construct firm paragraphs, (2) to vary their designs with varying situations, and (3) to create proper relationships among all the paragraphs in the total article, report, or chapter. In addition, the writer must strive to generate both reader interest and an appealing atmosphere within the paragraph itself.

Because of these exacting requirements, composing an acceptable paragraph demands your careful attention.

Function

The initial step in mastering the paragraph is to understand its true nature and function. A paragraph is essentially a *carefully developed body of thought* within the total piece of writing; it is a *group of sentences*, presented as a unit, *which treat a component* *part of the main idea.** The paragraph, therefore, is a principal division of the entire writing.

As is quite evident, the paragraph results from the necessity of dividing large subjects into smaller parts for analysis and discussion; it results from the logical practice of separating extensive questions or situations into lesser areas for detailed consideration. As he plans and develops his paragraphs, the writer is like the builder who, working from an overall blueprint, constructs a house section by section—relating each section, of course, to the others and to the central idea of erecting a family dwelling.

Another analogy commonly employed in explaining the paragraph relates the paragraph to one link in a chain. The writer must construct each paragraph as the ironsmith forges a chain; that is, he must so cast and join his paragraphs that, like the chain, the total writing can perform as a unit.

Once you comprehend the nature of the paragraph, you can understand an important statement about the place of the paragraph in the total unit of writing: in any extensive writing, the reader should sense a logical break in thought as he moves from paragraph to paragraph. He should feel that he is leaving one body of properly developed thought to move to another. Finally, after reading the entire work, he should see each paragraph as an integral part of the whole undertaking. Or, to return to the analogy of the house, he should feel that the writer, like the builder, has created a series of separate but related units—all essential to the complete project.

The preceding discussion treats the nature of the paragraph in a broad sense. You should note, however, that paragraphs often vary sharply according to (1) the nature of the writing (for example, narration versus exposition) and (2) the function of the particular paragraph (for example, introduction versus conclusion).

Furthermore, as will be shown in Chapter 9, the writer often selects a particular structure for a paragraph according to his view of the best way to handle the material. He may employ the thesis sentence, he may raise a question and answer it, or he may use one

---

*On some occasions, a writer sets off a single sentence as a paragraph in order to give strong emphasis to the thought therein. Obviously, such a sentence represents an exception to this statement.

of the other types of paragraphs presented in Chapter 9. Therefore, no precise formula can be devised for construction of all paragraphs. Each paragraph must reflect the writer's competence in dividing his main subject into parts and in developing each part in the form of a paragraph.

Below are two sets of two paragraphs. Each set reflects its author's dexterity in handling paragraph development. The first set is from one of America's most popular short stories; the second is from the 1935 edition of *An Economic Interpretation of the Constitution*.

In the first set, the author handles humorously and appealingly the composition of a group of personalities; in the second set, the author makes observations on the reception of the first edition of his book in 1913. In each instance, you can see a genuine proficiency in arranging details into a pleasing entity (the paragraph) and in relating the entities perfectly to each other.

● Times grew worse and worse with Rip Van Winkle as years of matrimony rolled on; a tart temper never mellows with age, and a sharp tongue is the only edged tool that grows keener with constant use. For a long while he used to console himself, when driven from home, by frequenting a kind of perpetual club of the sages, philosophers, and other idle personages of the village; which held its sessions on a bench before a small inn, designated by a rubicund portrait of His Majesty George the Third. Here they used to sit in the shade through a long lazy summer's day, talking listlessly over village gossip, or telling endless sleepy stories about nothing. But it would have been worth any statesman's money to have heard the profound discussions that sometimes took place, when by chance an old newspaper fell into their hands from some passing traveller. How solemnly they would listen to the contents, as drawled out by Derrick Van Brummel, the schoolmaster, a dapper learned little man, who was not to be daunted by the most gigantic word in the dictionary; and how sagely they would deliberate upon public events some months after they had taken place.

The opinions of this junto were completely controlled by Nicholas Vedder, a patriarch of the village, and landlord of the inn, at the door of which he took his seat from morning till night, just moving sufficiently to avoid the sun and keep in the shade of a large tree; so that the neighbors could tell the hour by his movements as accurately as by a sun-dial. It is true he was rarely heard to speak, but smoked his pipe incessantly. His adherents, however (for every great man has his adherents), perfectly understood him, and knew how to gather his opinions. When any thing that was read or related displeased him, he was observed to smoke his pipe vehemently, and to send forth short, frequent and angry puffs; but when pleased, he would inhale the smoke slowly and tranquilly, and emit it in light and placid clouds; and sometimes, taking his pipe from his mouth, and letting the fragrant vapor curl about his nose, would gravely nod his head in token of perfect approbation.   [Washington Irving, "Rip Van Winkle," 1819.]

- When my book appeared, it was roundly condemned by conservative Republicans, including ex-President Taft, and praised, with about the same amount of discrimination, by Progressives and others on the left wing. Perhaps no other book on the Constitution has been more severely criticized, and so little read. Perhaps no other book on the subject has been used to justify opinions and projects so utterly beyond its necessary implications. It was employed by a socialist writer to support a plea for an entirely new constitution and by a conservative judge of the United States Supreme Court to justify an attack on a new piece of "social legislation." Some members of the New York Bar Association became so alarmed by the book that they formed a committee and summoned me to appear before it; and, when I declined on the ground that I was not engaged in legal politics or political politics, they treated my reply as a kind of contempt of court. Few took the position occupied by Justice Oliver Wendell Holmes, who once remarked to me that he had not got excited about the book, like some of his colleagues, but had supposed that it was intended to throw light on the nature of the Constitution, and, in his opinion, did so in fact.

    Among my historical colleagues the reception accorded the volume varied. Professor William A. Dunning wrote me that he regarded it as "the pure milk of the word," although it would "make the heathen rage." Professor Albert Bushnell Hart declared that it was little short of indecent. Others sought to classify it by calling it "Marxian." Even as late as the year 1934, Professor Theodore Clarke Smith, in an address before the American Historical Association, expressed this view of the volume, in making it illustrative of a type of historical writing, which is "doctrinaire" and "excludes anything like impartiality." He said: "This is the view that American history, like all history, can and must be explained in economic terms. . . . This idea has its origin, of course, in the Marxian theories." Having made this assertion, Professor Smith turned his scholarly battery upon *An Economic Interpretation of the Constitution.* [Charles A. Beard, *An Economic Interpretation of the Constitution,* 1935.]

Content

Before you can develop a paragraph, you must decide on the material to be included and the arrangement of that material within the paragraph.

Any decisions regarding material to be included are fundamentally a matter of separating essential from nonessential detail. Any decisions regarding arrangement are a matter of determining the form that best suits the material. Sometimes these questions can be fairly simple, but they can also be thorny.

Although the problem of separating essential from nonessential material is considered extensively elsewhere, it nonetheless should be summarized here.* In description, exposition, and argument, the entire matter revolves about one question: What material is so clearly an integral part of this paragraph that omitting it would create a severe loss? In narration, the matter involves two questions: What material is clearly an integral part of the paragraph? What material contributes substantially to a desirable atmosphere?

---

*For narration, see p. 162; for description, see p. 166; for exposition, see p. 173; for argument, see p. 141.

Arrangement

The problem of arrangement of material has also been treated elsewhere. Yet once again, a few statements of summation can profitably be made here. The ideal situation is, obviously, to employ the arrangement that best suits the particular subject, and the writer must work constantly toward this ideal.

The most important consideration in arrangement must be a clearly discernible order. You must construct a pattern that eases reading, hence understanding. In short, you must construct your paragraph so that the reader can follow its development easily and comfortably. You can scarcely assemble and present your material in a trash basket arrangement.

Sometimes the matter of arrangement can be evolved by following a natural pattern. If, for example, you are to explain the operation of an assembly line, you face little or no problem in arranging your material. You simply recount the activity on the line from the first step to the last.* Similarly, you have no problem in arranging details in narrative writing; you merely treat them in their chronological order. (Some writers, however, depart from the chronological approach to narrative writing with good effect.)

On the other hand, many situations do not lend themselves to such convenient arrangements, and the writer faces problems in paragraph structure and content. The explanation of citizen reactions to a political petition, for instance, requires an analysis of the total situation, a classification of the reactions themselves, and some discussion of each reaction. Settling on an arrangement for this material is a complex task.

The paragraph below illustrates a skillful arrangement of details. The author has combined a narrative and a descriptive pattern to achieve an easy flowing, appealing style while he introduces the detail necessary to establish his central point.

● To be catapulted into megalopolis straight out of Arcadia is to be given a shock that may turn an innocent countryman into an

---

*See p. 100 for an example of this approach.

urban criminal lunatic. This was borne in on me when I was once hovering, in a helicopter, over the interior of Puerto Rico. From only a few hundred feet up, I was looking down at a choppy sea of jungle-covered hills with, here and there, a tiny clearing, containing just one cottage and one cornpatch. If I had been born and brought up in one of these secluded tropical homesteads, out of sight and hearing of the rush and roar of the modern urban world, how should I have felt if, under the spur of economic pressure, I had suddenly been transported into the East Side of New York City? Might I not have lost my moral bearings when, like a palm tree caught in a hurricane, I had been torn up from my social roots? I now understood why, in New York, some of the Puerto Rican immigrants make awkward neighbours for the better-acclimatized older inhabitants. I also appreciated the wisdom of the Puerto Rican Government's policy of seeking to create industrial employment at home for the redundant rural population of the island by offering to United States corporations attractive financial inducements to set up branch-factories in Puerto Rico. It might not be easy for a Puerto Rican peasant to accustom himself to living and working in San Juan; but the transition from agricultural to industrial work would at least be less upsetting for him if he were given the opportunity of making it without having to leave his native shores.   [Arnold J. Toynbee, *Change and Habit*, 1966.]

8.

Attributes
of the paragraph

Completeness

Above all, a well-developed paragraph must exhibit an aura of *completeness*. It must give the impression that the writer has searched into every corner and crevice for pertinent information; that he has deliberated properly upon every fact; and that he is now presenting that material in open and full form.

Below are two paragraphs that illustrate completeness. The first is a famous American writer's memory picture of a childhood experience. The second is a famous philosopher's comments on the mind of Josiah Royce, with whom he served in the department of philosophy at Harvard.

Notice how, in each instance, you have the feeling that the writer has presented a full account.

- I can see the farm yet, with perfect clearness. I can see all its belongings, all its details; the family room of the house, with a "trundle" bed in one corner and a spinning-wheel in another—a wheel whose rising and falling wail, heard from a distance, was the mournfulest of all sounds to me, and made me homesick and low spirited, and filled my atmosphere with the wandering spirits of the dead; the vast fireplace, piled high, on winter nights, with flaming hickory logs from whose ends a sugary sap bubbled out, but did not go to waste, for we scraped it off and ate it; the lazy cat spread out on the rough hearthstones; the drowsy dogs braced against the jambs and blinking; my aunt in one chimney corner, knitting; my uncle in the other, smoking his corn-cob pipe; the slick and carpetless oak floor faintly mirroring the dancing flame tongues and freckled with black indentations where fire coals had popped out and died a leisurely death; half a dozen children romping in the background twilight; "split"-bottomed chairs here and there, some with rockers; a cradle—out of service, but waiting, with confidence; in the early cold mornings a snuggle of children, in shirts and chemises, occupying the hearthstone and procrastinating—they could not bear to leave that comfortable place and go out on the wind-swept floor space between the house and kitchen where the general tin basin stood, and wash.   [Mark Twain, *Autobiography*, 1924.]

● Whatever the text-books and encyclopaedias could tell him, he knew; and if the impression he left on your mind was vague, that was partly because, in spite of his comprehensiveness, he seemed to view everything in relation to something else that remained untold. His approach to anything was oblique; he began a long way off, perhaps with the American preface of a funny story; and when the point came in sight, it was at once enveloped again in a cloud of qualifications, in the parliamentary jargon of philosophy. The tap once turned on, out flowed the stream of systematic disquisition, one hour, two hours, three hours of it, according to demand or opportunity. The voice, too, was merciless and harsh. You felt the overworked, standardised, academic engine, creaking and thumping on at the call of duty or of habit, with no thought of sparing itself or any one else.   [George Santayana, *Character & Opinion in the United States*, 1955.]

Capability

A second attribute of the well-developed paragraph is evidence of *capability* in the handling of ideas, thoughts, and argument; that is, the paragraph must reflect intellectual competence. There can be no errors in fact, no shortcomings in reasoning, and no inconsistencies in establishing conclusions. In short, the reader must feel that a good mind has handled the central thought.

Capability of this kind springs principally from a knowledge of the subject; yet it also arises from a special dexterity often identified as the "ability to handle facts." This is the ability demonstrated by the Aristotles and the Quintilians of classical antiquity and the Walter Lippmanns and the Edmund Wilsons of the present.

One important approach to capability is to check on the smaller aspects of your subject. Quite often, for example, you may fall victim to an unsound popular belief, or you may fail to test your statements for credibility. To appreciate this point, examine the passage below.

o When Mrs. Kittredge chanced to know at two or two-thirty in the morning that he was still at work, she would slip down and remind him that it was time for him to be getting some sleep. Very obediently he would go off to bed for the rest of the night. In the course of years, Mrs. Kittredge wearied a little of making the trip downstairs and had an electric bell installed with a button by her bed. But he did not like it. In the perfect quiet of night it made him jump. Sometimes nobody reminded him that he ought to be in bed, and he did not think of the matter himself; and when Thomas the chore man slipped into the study at six in the morning to build a new fire, there sat Professor Kittredge peacefully asleep in his comfortable chair before the empty fireplace, with one hand clutching a book on the arm of the chair as firmly as if he were awake. On such a night he did not get to bed at all. [Rollo Walter Brown, *Harvard Yard in the Golden Age*, 1948.]

In this selection, the author, a competent writer, is recounting how famed Harvard professor George Lyman Kittredge used to fall asleep while reading in the early hours of the morning. Despite the competence of the author and the general appeal of the passage, a rather serious question arises: Can a man in the throes of a long, deep sleep sit "clutching a book on the arm of the chair as firmly as if he were awake"? Anatomists and other specialists in the field of the human musculature would answer in the negative.

Unity

A third attribute of the well-developed paragraph is a *unity* of treatment. You must make sure that every thought is directly related to the central thought; you must check constantly for any digression, however slight; and you must be ever-mindful that each paragraph should be a supporting force for the entire writing.

Study the unity of treatment in the paragraph below.

● But the opposition to general education does not stem from causes located in the past alone. We are living in an age of specialism, in which the avenue to success for the student often lies in his choice of a specialized career, whether as a chemist, or an engineer, or a doctor, or a specialist in some form of business or of manual or technical work. Each of these specialties makes an increasing demand on the time and on the interest of the student. Specialism is the means for advancement in our mobile social structure; yet we must envisage the fact that a society controlled wholly by specialists is not a wisely ordered society. We cannot, however, turn away from specialism. The problem is how to save general education and its values within a system where specialism is necessary.   [The Harvard Committee, *General Education in a Free Society*, 1945.]

Coherence

A fourth attribute of the well-developed paragraph is *coherence*. Each sentence and each thought must be blended smoothly with the others, and each paragraph must be blended smoothly with the other paragraphs and with the central thought of the total writing.

Coherence in the paragraph is achieved by four principal means: (1) inversion, (2) transitional elements, (3) reference, and (4) organization of the total writing.

Inversion is discussed on page 25; organization of the total writing is discussed in Chapter 15. Therefore, we need only be concerned here with transitional elements and references.

Transitional elements are words and phrases that contribute to the smooth joining—commonly called "linkage"—of sentence with sentence and paragraph with paragraph.

Note, for example, the role of transitional elements in the short paragraphs below.

- Jim was quick but unreliable in his computations. Dave, *on the other hand*, was much slower but almost above error in his work—as were Bob and Chet. *In fact*, these three approached infallibility.

  Meanwhile, there was Marty, a rather dim-witted soul, who fell midway between these levels of accomplishment. He was just another laborer in the vineyard of Bellan, Jones, and Carter, Makers of Fine Clothes for Fine Men.

The term *reference* encompasses the use of pronouns, synonyms, and other devices employed to refer to a noun already cited. A skillful use of elements of reference can contribute greatly to smoothness of expression.

Note the use of elements of reference in the paragraph below.

- When Mr. Timkins was sixteen, *he* had a bad fall that injured his back severely. Nonetheless, this *determined man* continued to play tennis and to take long walks, and *he* exercised regularly to condition his muscles. *He* was, to be sure, *one* who would fight any obstacle that could be overcome by sheer effort—a *wounded combatant* but not a *defeated one*.

Fluency

The term *fluency* means "easy flow" or "uninterrupted movement." Hence fluency is a quality closely related to coherence.

To obtain fluency in a paragraph, you must work constantly for an easy, natural, smoothly flowing current; or stated negatively, you must eliminate any elements that hinder the reader's progress by making him pause to extract meaning.

Note, for instance, how smoothly the paragraph below moves.

● I left the woods for as good a reason as I went there. Perhaps it seemed to me that I had several more lives to live, and could not spare any more time for that one. It is remarkable how easily and insensibly we fall into a particular route, and make a beaten track for ourselves. I had not lived there a week before my feet wore a path from my door to the pond-side; and though it is five or six years since I trod it, it is still quite distinct. It is true, I fear, that others may have fallen into it, and so helped to keep it open. The surface of the earth is soft and impressible by the feet of men; and so with the paths which the mind travels. How worn and dusty, then, must be the highways of the world, how deep the ruts of tradition and conformity! I did not wish to take a cabin passage, but rather to go before the mast and on the deck of the world, for there I could best see the moonlight amid the mountains. I do not wish to go below now.   [Henry David Thoreau, *Walden*, 1854.]

Impediments to fluency can best be explained by illustration.

The passage below, taken from the famous Scottish essayist Thomas Carlyle, lacks fluency by modern standards. It is difficult to follow because of Carlyle's peculiar idiom and because of the sentence structure. The position of words, the inversions, and the overall construction make reading quite difficult.

○ All Works, each in their degree, are a making of Madness sane; —truly enough a religious operation; which cannot be carried on without religion. You have not work otherwise; you have eye-service, greedy grasping of wages, swift and ever swifter manufacture of semblances to get hold of wages. Instead of better felt-hats to cover your head, you have bigger lath-and-plaster hats set travelling the streets on wheels.   [*Past and Present*, 1843.]

The following paragraph, a stenographic record of a college dean's short speech to a student, lacks fluency because of the excessive use of subordination and interpolation.

o   What, may I ask, did you, his friend, I believe, if you can tell me, although you probably won't want to say, think as he shouted, not once I am told, but several times, at the officer who is, you may be sure, a friend of every student in this college?

The following paragraph, extracted from a student book review, lacks fluency because of the absence of transitional elements and the generally rough-edged movement of the whole writing.

o   In *The American*, Henry James takes a representative American, Christopher Newman, and places him in a society which can neither understand nor accept his way of living. He attempts to contrast American idealism with French realism, the latter seemingly corrupt to Newman, and succeeds. James dedicates himself to the defense of the salient virtues of his countrymen. Newman is the outsider with self-confidence and easy assurance, and the Bellegarde family resists his intrusion. He becomes much more than the representative American as the story progresses, however.

Pace

The term *pace* refers to the speed with which a specific passage moves. It designates the tempo that the reader feels in a given sentence, paragraph, or selection.

Readers, of course, become familiar with pace in their earliest years. They realize in their beginning school days that limericks have a rapid pace. For instance:

●   There was an old man from Nantucket
Who kept all his cash in a bucket.
A daughter named Nan ran away with a man
And as for the bucket
Nantucket.

These same readers, meanwhile, become vaguely aware that the pace of short stories is much slower. They experience a certain calm, thoughtful movement as they follow the many stories that begin, "Once upon a time."

For you, the importance of pace lies in the fact that you must learn how to adjust the pace to your subject. A long, leisurely essay, such as one by a James Russell Lowell or an Oliver Wendell Holmes, which treats a philosophical topic, must have a slow, deliberate pace. On the other hand, a description of a battle—as in Hemingway's *For Whom the Bell Tolls*—requires a much faster pace. In each instance, of course, the nature of the material determines the pace to be employed.

The paragraphs below represent a number of sharply different paces. Note the differences in subject matter and the differences in stylistic devices as they relate to the pace of each selection.

- The oceans are man's last frontier on this planet. To conserve the purity of their wilderness and the mystery of their wildlife while industrialization is sprawling farther and farther out, deeper and deeper down, is no small task. Mankind, pushed off the edge of overcrowded continents, finds itself at a turning point in its evolution. Advanced technology enables man to return to his pristine nature. The highest mammal on the scale of natural evolution, he has been made by cultural evolution with its technology into a clumsy, rapacious bird; now, technology is devising artificial gills for him, so he can be made fish again, and breathe and live down there where life began.   [Elisabeth Mann Borgese, "Who Owns the Oceans?" *VISTA*, January/February 1972.]

The pace of the above passage is slow because of the aphoristic nature of the writing and the challenge each sentence presents to the reader's thought processes. The reader must proceed slowly because he must reflect carefully on the thought in each sentence.

- Genealogies are rarely accurate. Their most usual purpose is, after all, to discover eminent ancestors, and a sense of veracity is not likely to inhibit such an enterprise. Social pretensions are too important to let the truth interfere with them. The Homeric heroes who boasted of divine ancestors to secure "sanction for aristocratic privilege" were neither the first nor the last noblemen to embellish their family trees. Indeed Homer's thoroughly aristocratic gods were no less prone to display their pedigrees. However, if divine ancestors are the ultimate source of honor, it ineluctably follows that vulgar and disreputable ones are an intolerable disgrace. The traditional vocabulary of insult reveals nothing more clearly. To abuse a man's relatives and ancestors is the surest way of impugning his dignity and of assaulting his social position. That is why genealogies can serve as readily to destroy as to enhance claims to social supremacy. [Judith N. Shklar, "Subversive Genealogies," *Daedalus*, Winter 1972.]

The paragraph above has a slow pace because of the adroit mixture of subtle humor and depth of thought. The reader must peruse each sentence thoroughly if he is to derive the full force of the passage.

● In last November's issue we argued the inappropriateness of referring to our society as a melting pot. The melting-pot idea does not work, because most persons want to preserve their identity rather than be melted down and remolded. A better analogy for our pluralistic society is the salad bowl, in which the various ingredients form a unified whole, but at the same time are clearly identifiable.   [Editorial, *The Instructor*, March 1972.]

In this passage, the pace is rapid. This results from the writer's use of a style that resembles rather closely the language of a fluent, knowledgeable conversationalist. To appreciate this particular point, you need only read the passage aloud, as though it were a radio or a television script. This experiment will reveal the ease with which the sentences flow and the overall speed with which the paragraph moves.

● Visitors to Panama have much to be enthusiastic about. The scuba diving is superb. The beaches are incomparable. Fisher-men call it the blue marlin capital of the world. There are lovely, hidden coves and lonely, quiet places for those who want to get away from it all.

And Panama is the land where molas come from.

Molas are the brightly-colored, design-covered cloth panels made by the Cuna Indians of the San Blas Islands, just off the coast of Panama. Tourists have "discovered" molas, and although their cost in Panama may be only a few dollars, they command far higher prices in New York. The reason for their popularity is not hard to find. Molas are delightful in design and color. They make unusual souvenirs, and often they are works of art as well.   [Roy Klotz, "The Mola: Artistry in Cloth," *Design*, Midwinter 1972.]

The pace of the above passage is quite fast because of the simply constructed, short sentences which, at times, are almost staccato in their effect. The direct, conversational tone of the writing also carries the reader along at a rapid tempo.

● Dr. Timothy Costello, then a professor at New York University, was conducting a class one October day when he noticed a familiar face at the door. Dr. Costello invited the man in and urged him to take over the class. For over an hour, the newcomer happily discussed the problems of city politics and management with the students. He was uniquely qualified to discuss the subject, for he was John Lindsay, soon to become mayor of New York City and a nationally known spokesman on the problems of cities. Incidentally, Lindsay later appointed his faculty host that day to the post of Deputy Mayor.   [Herbert B. Livesey, *Anyone Can Go to College*, 1971.]

This paragraph displays a mixture of pace. Notice how the writer moves slowly and deliberately in order to create suspense and then surprise his reader. Notice, also, the impact he gains by hurrying the thought expressed in the last sentence.

Proportion

The term *proportion*, broadly speaking, refers to the relative emphases accorded the various details in a paragraph or the larger points of the total writing.

The writer's points in an argument, for example, are usually of relatively equal importance and so are developed at relatively equal length. Therefore, in a carefully wrought piece, you naturally sense in the paragraphs a certain similarity or evenness of development. However, when one point is more significant or less significant than another, it is developed to a greater or lesser degree. This process of extending or limiting development according to relative importance is a matter of proportion.

Once again, there is no final guide for finding the right balance. You can only try to invoke a critical judgment that will prevent your overdeveloping or underdeveloping your paragraphs by examining the central idea of the paragraph carefully and striving to accord it its proper proportion.

Note the skillful handling of proportion in the paragraphs below.

● The controversy about violence on television is rich in rhetoric but generally short on fact. The report as published on Thursday by the BBC audience research department is therefore a useful contribution to the debate. It is two studies in one; the first is an attempt to assess how much violence is shown on British screens, and the second tries to characterize viewers' reactions to it. Starting with a definition of violence as "any act(s) which may cause physical and/or psychological injury, hurt, or death to persons, animals, or property, whether intentional or accidental," the BBC asked 105 specially selected viewers to analyze samples of BBC and Independent television programmes over a period of 21 weeks, noting and classifying violence and its frequency.

　The sample covered a wide range of programmes, but, not surprisingly, the survey found that violence on television was almost wholly confined to news, current affairs, and what is broadly described as fictional drama. Nor is it any shock to learn that violent episodes are seen far more often in news bulletins than elsewhere—10.4 incidents per hour compared with an overall average on all channels of 2.2. On the other hand, only a quarter of those violent incidents reported on the news were presented visually. [Editorial, *The Economist*, January 29, 1972.]

● White workers tend to see blacks as threatening their jobs when in fact their jobs are being threatened by automation and cybernation. Instead of accepting the technical progress of automation and using it as a basis to demand the right to a decent livelihood for everyone, working or not, they have chosen the road of fighting blacks not only on the job market but even in other arenas involving the black community, such as schools and police, where white workers are not directly threatened. Often afraid to confront blacks at the point of production, they organize outside the plant with the aim of inflaming not only white workers but other groups in the white population not engaged in the process of production. Thus, side by side with the development of the black revolutionary forces are growing the counterrevolutionary forces of white workers. [James Boggs, "A Black View of the White Worker," 1970.]

Atmosphere

Atmosphere is one of the most important yet difficult qualities to handle in the writing of the paragraph. For better or for worse, every sentence, every paragraph, every unit of writing has an atmosphere; and the writing is successful, among other considerations, in direct proportion to the appeal of that atmosphere. This highly enigmatic quality has long been recognized and respected by important writers. Yet it remains a baffling matter. You can only sense its presence and note its absence.

Below are the opening passages of a chapter from a well-known American novel. The author has created successfully the atmosphere that arises from the special kind of weariness experienced with long travel under uncomfortable and enervating circumstances.

● Under the rolling clouds of the prairie a moving mass of steel. An irritable clank and rattle beneath a prolonged roar. The sharp scent of oranges cutting the soggy smell of unbathed people and ancient baggage.

Towns as planless as a scattering of pasteboard boxes on an attic floor. The stretch of faded gold stubble broken only by clumps of willows encircling white houses and red barns.

No. 7, the way-train, grumbling through Minnesota, imperceptibly climbing the giant tableland that slopes in a thousand-mile rise from hot Mississippi bottoms to the Rockies.

It is September, hot, very dusty.

There is no smug Pullman attached to the train, and the day coaches of the East are replaced by free chair cars, with each seat cut into two adjustable plush chairs, the head-rests covered with doubtful linen towels. Halfway down the car is a semi-partition of carved oak columns, but the aisle is of bare, splintery, grease-blackened wood. There is no porter, no pillows, no provision for beds, but all today and all tonight they will ride in this long steel box—farmers with perpetually tired wives and children who seem all to be of the same age; workmen going to new jobs; traveling salesmen with derbies and freshly shined shoes.

They are parched and cramped, the lines of their hands filled with grime; they go to sleep curled in distorted attitudes, heads against the window-panes or propped on rolled coats on seat-arms, and legs thrust into the aisle. They do not read; apparently they do not think. They wait. An early-wrinkled, young-old mother, moving as though her joints were dry, opens a suitcase in which are seen creased blouses, a pair of slippers worn through at the toes, a bottle of patent medicine, a tin cup, a paper-covered book about dreams which the news-butcher has coaxed her into buying. She brings out a graham cracker which she feeds to a baby lying flat on a seat and wailing hopelessly. Most of the crumbs drop on the red plush of the seat, and the woman sighs and tries to brush them away, but they leap up impishly and fall back on the plush.   [Sinclair Lewis, *Main Street*, 1920.]

In evaluating the atmosphere of a given paragraph, you must rely on innate judgment, aided by cultivated critical ability. You can begin to develop this ability by asking yourself a simple question of every piece of writing you encounter: What kind of personality does this writing reflect? Is it overbearing, conceited, repulsive, pleasant, charming, appealing?

What is the atmosphere, for example, in each of the three paragraphs below? Read each paragraph thoughtfully before reading the comment that follows.

- It seems our city's mayor has taken the song "Age of Aquarius" to heart. "Let the sun shine, let the sun shine" are the words that could be used to paraphrase any of His Honor's recent speeches, news releases, and press conferences. Our schools are foundering as a result of administrative inefficiency; the municipal budget is badly out of balance; and crime in the streets is increasing alarmingly. Yet our mayor announces reassuringly that our city is "nearly perfect."

This paragraph reflects an atmosphere of exasperation and sarcasm. As his careful phrasing reveals, the writer is more than merely annoyed; he is seriously concerned about a situation that he finds genuinely bad. And in measured but satirical tones, he is calling for action.

- Everything was being done in the inherited Swedish tradition. Herring was soaked and pickled, and cranberry steamed and bubbled over on the black stove. The aroma of hot sweet breads and sugar cakes, steaming rice pudding and juicy Swedish meatballs, and the buttered goose mixed in the air with bayberry, spice, and pine. The Scotch pine stood proud and heavy with shining white candles and homemade ornaments, and the wood and straw manger with its many painted figures awaited the arrival of its King.

The first sentence of this paragraph sets the stage for the details that follow—all with the aim of capturing the prevailing atmosphere of the occasion. Although the writing is somewhat heavy, the selection achieves its purpose rather well.

- The Harrisburg Hounds are not one of the best basketball teams to appear on the hoop scene in recent years. They are not even a very good team. However, behind their somewhat crude passing, unimpressive ball handling, low averages, and general lack of luster stands a very unusual purpose: they are inmates of the Dauphin County Prison, engaging in the first stage of an experimental program in rehabilitation of prisoners.

The atmosphere of this paragraph is calm, thoughtful, and restrained. This tone accentuates the writer's conviction that the whole idea of such a program merits our support.

Rhythm

The matter of *rhythm* assumes special importance in the writing of the paragraph because of its role in contributing to readability. Just as the individual sentence should be characterized by an appealing rhythm, so the paragraph should have a pleasing pattern of rising and falling, a pleasant cadence. It should carry its reader along in the current of its movement without any jarring or interruptive effect.

To ensure the presence of rhythm, you should read your sentences to yourself, watching especially for the overall movement of the paragraph. You should strive to produce writing that "reads itself."

Here is a paragraph that illustrates the presence of an appealing rhythmic quality.

- The boys loved Lime and made him their hero at once. His face was almost always shining with a smile, and his blue eyes gleamed good-naturedly on man and beast. His voice was so soft and low it expressed weakness, or at least laziness, but it was in truth a very deceptive peculiarity. He knew no poetry or history, could barely cipher out the price of a load of barley, and had not travelled much, and yet he never uttered a word that was not, somehow, interesting to his hearers. Part of this was due to his natural reticence, and part to his manner of speech, which made even a statement of fact worth listening to.   [Hamlin Garland, *Boy Life on the Prairie*, 1885.]

9.

The structure of the paragraph

In constructing a paragraph, you may employ any one of several fundamental patterns. Each pattern naturally offers certain advantages that make it especially appropriate for specific situations. By mastering the patterns and learning when to use them, you should be able to attain the level of those seasoned writers for whom the development of the paragraph has become largely a natural process. Topflight writers of fiction, for example, give only limited thought to the creation of a paragraph; they are able to place their material into appropriate paragraphs without apparent effort. Similarly, competent professional report writers have little difficulty with paragraphing because the procedure has become almost habitual.

On the following pages the most commonly employed paragraph structures are presented. You should first become thoroughly familiar with each of these basic structures. Thereafter, you should attempt to incorporate them into your own writing as the particular writing situation may demand.

Thesis sentence

The thesis, or topic, sentence is the most common of all devices employed in the development of paragraphs. When you employ this device, you state your central thought in the form of a single sentence at the opening of the paragraph and then enlarge upon, substantiate, or develop that thought in the remaining sentences.

For example, the statement

Sailing a small craft in the midst of choppy seas is a difficult undertaking.

can serve as a thesis sentence for a paragraph that explains why the undertaking is difficult. The writer, of course, constructs his paragraph by substantiating or supporting this initial statement.

In drafting a thesis sentence, you must choose your words carefully. Regard the thesis sentence as the essence of everything to follow; that is, understand its role as the unifying element and the main support of the entire paragraph.

Below are two paragraphs that illustrate the thesis-sentence construction.

- Travelling is a fool's paradise. Our first journeys discover to us the indifference of places. At home I dream that at Naples, at Rome, I can be intoxicated with beauty and lose my sadness. I pack my trunk, embrace my friends, embark on the sea, and at last wake up in Naples, and there beside me is the stern fact, the sad self, unrelenting, identical, that I fled from. I seek the Vatican and palaces. I affect to be intoxicated with sights and suggestions, but I am not intoxicated. My giant goes with me wherever I go. [Ralph Waldo Emerson, "Self-Reliance," 1840.]

- As a matter of fact, the educated man uses at least three languages. With his family and his close friends, on the ordinary, unimportant occasions of daily life, he speaks, much of the time, a monosyllabic sort of shorthand. On more important occasions and when dealing with strangers in his official or business relations, he has a more formal speech, more complete, less allusive, politely qualified, wisely reserved. In addition he has some acquaintance with the literary speech of his language. He understands this when he reads it, and often enjoys it, but he hesitates to use it. In times of emotional stress hot fragments of it may come out of him like lava, and in times of feigned emotion, as when giving a commencement address, cold, greasy gobbets of it will ooze forth.   [Bergen Evans, "Grammar for Today," *The Atlantic*, March 1960.]

The thesis sentence need not be the first sentence in the paragraph. In the paragraph below, for example, it is actually the third. The first sentence acts as a transitional element to join the paragraph with the one preceding it; the second sentence raises a question; and the third or topic sentence then presents the thesis of the paragraph.

- If a prospect is not a prophecy, it is a view. What does the world of the arts and sciences look like? There are two ways of looking at it: One is the view of the traveler, going by horse or foot, from village to village to town, staying in each to talk with those who live there and to gather something of the quality of its life. This is the intimate view, partial, somewhat accidental, limited by the limited life and strength and curiosity of the traveler, but intimate and human, in a human compass. The other is the vast view, showing the earth with its fields and towns and valleys as they appear to a camera carried in a high-altitude rocket. In one sense this prospect will be more complete; one will see all branches of knowledge, one will see all the arts, one will see them as part of the vastness and complication of the whole of human life on earth. But one will miss a great deal; the beauty and warmth of human life will largely be gone from that prospect.   [J. Robert Oppenheimer, *The Open Mind*, 1955.]

Implied thesis

Sometimes a paragraph can be developed by the use of sentences that imply rather than state the central thought or thesis of the paragraph.

Note how the author of the passage below does not state flatly his intention of defining when men are and are not free. Rather, he presents his definition by implication.

● Men are less free than they imagine; ah, far less free. The freest are perhaps least free.

Men are free when they are in a living homeland, not when they are straying and breaking away. Men are free when they are obeying some deep, inward voice of religious belief. Obeying from within. Men are free when they belong to a living, organic, *believing* community, active in fulfilling some unfulfilled, perhaps unrealized purpose. Not when they are escaping to some wild west. The most unfree souls go west, and shout of freedom. Men are freest when they are most unconscious of freedom. The shout is a rattling of chains, always was.

Men are not free when they are doing just what they like. The moment you can do just what you like, there is nothing you care about doing. Men are only free when they are doing what the deepest self likes.   [D. H. Lawrence, *Studies in Classic American Literature*, 1964.]

Question and answer

The question-and-answer paragraph is one in which the opening sentence raises a question that the ensuing sentences then answer. Thus, the paragraph is developed by presenting a set of facts or a viewpoint that answers the question.

Below are examples of the question-and-answer paragraph.

● What is the role of television? It's difficult to define. At its most ordinary it acts as an extension of vision. It relays routine information, routine entertainment, routine education, into the drawing rooms of the audience. At its best it bestows insight. It heightens perception, reveals new relationships, and brings with it a new view of our daily lives.   [Aubrey Singer, "Television: Window on Culture or Reflection in the Glass?" *American Scholar*, Spring 1966.]

- When I am asked how much *All the King's Men* owes to the actual politics of Louisiana in the 30's, I can only be sure that if I had never gone to live in Louisiana and if Huey Long had not existed, the novel would never have been written. But this is far from saying that my "state" in *All the King's Men* is Louisiana (or any of the other forty-nine stars in our flag), or that my Willie Stark is the late Senator. What Louisiana and Senator Long gave me was a line of thinking and feeling that did eventuate in the novel.   [Robert Penn Warren, "*All the King's Men:* The Matrix of Experience," *Yale Review*, 1963.]

- An American automobilist once complained to me, "Your Paris traffic regulations just don't make sense. Why don't you make all the streets one-way, with alternate east and west traffic, the way we do in New York? That would solve all your problems." Of course it would, in theory. But he had forgotten that it took 17 centuries to build Paris, and it can hardly be converted into an American gridiron overnight, even if we so desired.   [André Maurois, "Why Europeans Criticize the U.S.A.," *Reader's Digest*, January 1963.]

Definition

Sometimes a paragraph can be developed by defining an important term or phrase. The term or phrase appears in the opening sentence, and thereafter the paragraph concentrates on presenting a definition. In the paragraph below, for example, the main function is to define the phrase "good editorial page."

- A good editorial page will have a credo of principles through which it speaks to its readers. It will give them an opportunity to talk back through letters to the editor. It will vary its tone, speaking neither in a sustained whisper nor a sustained scream. It will guard against prefabricated, flannel-suited opinions that soon become flannel-mouthed opinions. It will be receptive to new ideas and will question old concepts. It will cherish its independence and will be wary of a narrow and automatic conformity. It will avoid becoming the mouthpiece only of particular segments of that society, and it will recognize the inconsistency between fair comment three years out of four and partisan atavism at election time. It will understand that this is a great and growing country which cannot be measured by old *status quo* yardsticks.   [Robert H. Estabrook, "What Is a Responsible Press?" Address delivered at the University of Michigan, December 1959.]

In the paragraph above, the author chose the paragraph of definition to express his ideas regarding a good editorial page. In other instances, however, the paragraph of definition becomes a necessity, rather than an option, because the writer is using an unfamiliar term or because he is assigning a limited meaning to a standard term. The passage below, for instance, is the opening paragraph in the work cited. Here the author defines his central term with the bluntness of a dictionary definition.

● Tribalism is the practice of the belief that one's own tribe is better than or superior to the tribes of others. It is a belief which is supported and reinforced by sacred rites and secular rituals, serving to identify the members with the group in peace, and to unify the whole tribe in times of stress or conflict. Not all human populations are tribes, and not all tribes consider themselves to be better than or superior to other peoples. [Ashley Montagu, "On Tribalism Today," *VISTA*, November/December 1968.]

Analysis

The paragraph of analysis is closely related to the paragraph of definition. In fact, it is so closely related that the line between them is often arbitrary.

In developing a paragraph by analysis, you make a statement at the opening of the paragraph and then proceed to analyze the implications of the statement; in this sense the development resembles quite closely that of the thesis sentence paragraph.

Below are two examples of the paragraph of analysis. The first is by one of the most widely respected American sociologists of the twentieth century. The second is one of the most frequently quoted of all passages on the nature of work. It is the seriocomic pronouncement by Cyril Northcote Parkinson, British political scientist and historian—a pronouncement that has made famous the phrase, "Parkinson's Law."

- Nowadays men often feel that their private lives are a series of traps. They sense that within their everyday worlds, they cannot overcome their troubles, and in this feeling, they are often quite correct: What ordinary men are directly aware of and what they try to do are bounded by the private orbits in which they live; their visions and their powers are limited to the close-up scenes of job, family, neighborhood; in other milieux, they move vicariously and remain spectators. And the more aware they become, however vaguely, of ambitions and of threats which transcend their immediate locales, the more trapped they seem to feel.   [C. Wright Mills, *The Sociological Imagination*, 1956.]

- Work expands so as to fill the time available for its completion. General recognition of this fact is shown in the proverbial phrase "It is the busiest man who has time to spare." Thus an elderly lady of leisure can spend the entire day in writing and dispatching a postcard to her niece at Bognor Regis. An hour will be spent in finding the postcard, another in hunting for spectacles, half an hour in a search for the address, an hour and a quarter in composition, and twenty minutes in deciding whether or not to take an umbrella when going to the mailbox in the next street. The total effort that would occupy a busy man for three minutes all told may in this fashion leave another person prostrate after a day of doubt, anxiety, and toil. [*Parkinson's Law and Other Studies in Administration*, 1957.]

Comparison or contrast

In many instances, the nature of a particular point or the character of a given object can best be made clear by employing a comparison or a contrast.

When, for example, a lecturer describes a crocodile, he must, of necessity, distinguish it from an alligator. When a tennis instructor wants to explain how to swing a racket, he must compare the right way with the wrong way. When a meteorologist details a freakish change in the weather, he must contrast the abnormal with the normal.

In instances such as these, you will usually find that the comparison or contrast paragraph becomes the most expedient approach. You simply proceed by relating the situation to be described or explained to a situation that provides an appropriate basis for comparison or contrast.

You will find the comparison or contrast approach easy to employ. Most speakers and writers use it naturally every day. When a person says, for example,

Loper was a pedestrian writer; he was not a great author.

he is, of course, employing a contrast to make his point. When this same speaker writes a paragraph in this vein, he is merely extending the pattern.

Note how, in the paragraph below, the author explains the temperament and approach of the painter of today by making a comparison.

● The temperament and approach to his work of the painter today seems to be very much the same as that of the painter of the past. Patience, skill, and devotion were not a monopoly of the older masters, nor are haste and inferior workmanship the necessary characteristics of the moderns. We today are apt to judge the work of the past by its cream, which has survived on museum and gallery walls; but anyone who has had experience of old collections, or frequents auction sales will realize how much inferior work was produced in the past, quite apart from the immense amount that has deservedly perished. Similarly, early painters are sometimes credited with a knowledge and learning they never possessed. For example, art historians have been known to search the classics for explanation of a subject, implying that the painter had not only a knowledge of Greek and Latin, but time to make use of it; while the true source was a textbook of the painter's own day, the then equivalent of, say, Bulfinch's *Age of Fable*.   [W. G. Constable, *The Painter's Workshop*, 1963.]

In the following paragraph, the author makes his point more by the use of contrast than by the use of comparison.

● Yet this refinement of terminology is not enough to show up the distinctiveness of the sociological angle of vision. We may get closer by comparing the latter with the perspective of other disciplines concerned with human actions. The economist, for example, is concerned with the analyses of processes that occur in society and that can be described as social. These processes have to do with the basic problem of economic activity—the allocation of scarce goods and services within a society. The economist will be concerned with these processes in terms of the way in which they carry out, or fail to carry out, this function. The sociologist, in looking at the same processes, will naturally have to take into consideration their economic purpose. But his distinctive interest is not necessarily related to this purpose as such. He will be interested in a variety of human relationships and interactions that may occur here and that may be quite irrelevant to the economic goals in question. Thus economic activity involves relationships of power, prestige, prejudice or even play that can be analyzed with only marginal reference to the properly economic function of the activity. [Peter L. Berger, *Invitation to Sociology*, 1963.]

The paragraph below, extracted from the writings of one of contemporary America's best known commentators on current affairs, makes its point by a use of both comparison and contrast.

● We miss the whole point when we imagine that we tolerate the freedom of our political opponents as we tolerate a howling baby next door, as we put up with the blasts from our neighbor's radio because we are too peaceable to heave a brick through the window. If this were all there is to freedom of opinion, that we are too good-natured or too timid to do anything about our opponents and our critics except to let them talk, it would be difficult to say whether we are tolerant because we are magnanimous or because we are lazy, because we have strong principles or because we lack serious convictions, whether we have the hospitality of an inquiring mind or the indifference of an empty mind. And so, if we truly wish to understand why freedom is necessary in a civilized society, we must begin by realizing that, because freedom of discussion improves our own opinions, the liberties of other men are our own vital necessity.   [Walter Lippmann, "The Indispensable Opposition," *The Atlantic*, August 1939.]

Successive steps

When you write of any formal or well-established procedure, the successive-step development of the paragraph can generally be employed. As the name implies, this paragraph details a procedure or process in a series of steps.

For example, if you are to explain an election system, you can begin by explaining how the nominees are determined; thereafter you can explain how the voting is carried out, how the results are tallied, and how the winners are determined. In short, you simply follow the pattern of the events themselves.

Below are two examples of successive-step paragraph development. The first is a direct use of the technique; the second combines the successive-step procedure with an expository approach.

● The experiment was conducted under regular school conditions, and the teachers, who were accustomed to a data-collecting principal, were not informed that anything special was going on. Teachers used their customary method of teaching spelling, the test-study method. The words for the week were presented on Monday. The words were pronounced, used in a sentence, and defined if necessary. Students spelled the word and, after the test was corrected, added their misspellings to their "demon" list. Words missed were studied on Tuesday. A second test was given on Wednesday, and missed words were studied on Thursday. After a third test on Friday, each student recorded his mistakes for further study the following week. Reviews were held every fourth week. Students were urged to study spelling by pronouncing a word, visualizing the syllabicated word with eyes closed, recalling the word, looking at the word, writing the word, comparing the word, writing it again, comparing it again, and writing it a third and last time.   [J. Stephen Sherwin, *Four Problems in Teaching English*, 1969.]

- Here is how the station works. The Leach Packmaster trucks are weighed and then dump their loads on a concrete apron. Two one cubic-yard wheel loaders, a Massey-Ferguson MF 11 and a Michigan, move the refuse into a ground level hopper. The refuse then drops into the Bowles hydraulic compaction unit which has a total packing pressure of 90,000 pounds. The compression chamber is six feet long, six feet high, and three feet wide. Mounted on a concrete foundation, the hydraulic packing mechanism has a nine-inch diameter double acting hydraulic cylinder with a seven-foot stroke attached to a packing blade three feet high and six feet wide. The hydraulic unit has a 90-gallon-per-minute vane hydraulic pump driven by a 60 horsepower motor and a 300-gallon hydraulic fluid reservoir. The piston and packing blade mechanisms are electrically controlled to operate at three cycles per minute. Both can be operated manually.   [Bartlett L. Kennedy, "Refuse Transfer Station, Santa Monica," *Western City Magazine*, February 1972.]

Point-by-point development

Quite similar to the successive-step process is the point-by-point development of a paragraph. Under this procedure, the writer moves from one point to the next in order to develop his main idea.

If, for instance, you are to write of the requirements for scuba diving, you could easily develop your paragraph by speaking of the importance of sound physical condition, swimming ability, and desire. As you come to each point, you merely explain its role in achieving success in this fast-growing sport.

Notice how the author of the paragraph below employs the point-by-point process to explain how the United States entered World War I.

● What actually effected the transition from legal neutrality to practical belligerence in 1917 was the war situation, prepared by Mr. Wilson with his first stand on the submarine and set, as it were, by the emotional shock of the *Lusitania*. The President was able to postpone the crisis for some two years by forcing upon the Germans a long series of compromises and partial surrenders. Although the submarines managed to torpedo many vessels and kill a considerable number of American citizens in the course of this correspondence, the Germans never forced the President to abandon his fundamental position. From the *Lusitania* crisis until the declaration of unrestricted submarine warfare on February 1, 1917, Mr. Wilson emerged substantially successful from each incident that arose. It was in this way that he avoided war. But each success only made a subsequent retreat more difficult for him; as time went on he became more and more the prisoner of his own victories. [Walter Millis, "How We Entered the Last One," *The New Republic*, July 31, 1935.]

Effect to cause

In the effect-to-cause paragraph, the opening sentence makes a statement regarding an effect; the remaining sentences in the paragraph then detail the causes that lead to the particular effect. For instance, a typical opening sentence—the statement of effect—can be,

Today's college graduates are sharply different from those of twenty-five years ago.

The remaining sentences in the paragraph then proceed to explain the reasons behind the statement.

Below are examples of the effect-to-cause paragraph.

- One interesting index of this is the decline of evening dress, especially among men, and conversely, the invasion of the office by sports clothes. This looks like an offshoot of the cult of effortlessness, and of course men say "it's too much trouble" in explaining why they don't change for dinner or the evening. But the explanation lies rather in the fact that most men today simply do not know how to change roles, let alone mark the change by proper costuming. Another reason may be the fear of being thought high-hat; one can wear gaudy shirts but not stiff ones. Thus the sport shirt and casual dress show that one is a good fellow not only on the golf course or on vacation but in the office and at dinner too.   [David Riesman, *The Lonely Crowd*, 1961.]

- Gauged by CU's recent test projects, the makers of portable electric heaters have little to boast about in the safety record of their products. In our 1965 report, more than one-third of the heaters tested flunked our tests for fire, heat or electrical hazards. In 1969, we rated more than half of the heaters in our project Not Acceptable for similar reasons. The 1973 picture? A failure rate of one out of every two for potential hazards, as the box on page 641 details. That's a sorry comment on an appliance whose very nature demands the utmost in careful design.   ["Portable Electric Heaters," *Consumer Reports*, October 1973.]

Cause to effect

Naturally, the effect-to-cause paragraph must be associated directly with the cause-to-effect paragraph. Obviously, in the cause-to-effect paragraph, the cause is stated in the opening sentences and the effects are then detailed in the succeeding sentences.

- It's easy to visualize the kind of institution that would result from putting together an administrative officer who simulates the role of educational leader, a faculty made up of those who simulate the role of the scholar-teacher and an enrollment made up of young men and women who simulate the role of students. You would have a simulated college or university—but if it is done as cleverly as Madison Avenue has done many things, many, many people will think it is the real thing.   [John C. Warner, "The Fine Art of Simulation," *Carnegie Alumnus*, April 1959.]

● The fact in broadcasting, for instance, is that what enters the microphone with the speed of sound travels to the ends of the earth at the speed of light, so that a hundred million people may hear it simultaneously and may never hear anything to challenge what they have heard. The fact in the movies is that the film can be endlessly duplicated and can produce emotional disturbances in widely separated crowds of people who have no chance to balance any other influence against it. The availability of these forms and of the comic books, the amount of time that can be spent on them, the negligible demand they make on the purse and the mind, are new phenomena in the world; their capacity to affect the lives of people who never see or hear them is the result we get when we multiply these new factors. A new social force has been created by high-speed printing presses and by the power driven projector and by the electronic system, which may master all the other mechanics of the entertainment industry. [Archibald MacLeish, "The Poet and the Press," *The Atlantic*, March 1959.]

The unusual stylistic device

On rare occasions, a writer may find an opportunity to build a paragraph around the use of an unusual stylistic device.

Essentially, the writer seeks to capitalize upon the impact novelty can provide; he seeks to obtain the force created by departing from the conventional.

Note how, stylistically speaking, each of the paragraphs below departs from conventional paragraph structures.

- Arrest and convict them? Stop their sources of supply? Seek to cure them? Support their habits by a public supply system? Root out the sources of their sickness? Focus on their life-style?
  I am speaking, of course, about drug users and pushers and the debate about causes, cures, and punishments.   [Max Lerner, newspaper column, March 27, 1972.]

- Conservation. It's been a popular catchword for the last few years. But what does it mean? Among the many organizations around the world qualified to tell you, the San Diego Zoo in California is preeminent—and the zoo is up to something new.   [Robert H. Rufa, *Travel*, February 1972.]

- Ecology! Environmental protection! Recycle your cans! These are cries heard 'round the nation these days. Environmentalists want everything possible to be recycled so our nation won't become one great trash heap of empty cartons, waste paper, cans, bottles, and junked appliances.   ["Minireports," *Consumer Bulletin*, April 1972.]

- Readin', 'ritin', and 'rithmetic—in fact all the subjects in the curriculum—held the attention of students during the 1970's as never before. People in the United States achieved higher educational levels than in any previous decade.   ["Trends," *Today's Education*, February–March 1982.]

- Where will you be working in 1990? In sales? Construction? Health care? If you haven't mulled over these questions, perhaps now is as good a time as any since you in a sense will be competing with 119 million other workers by 1990. Also, new technologies will both *create* and *eliminate* hundreds of thousands of jobs.   [Alex Poinsett, *Ebony*, March 1982.]

Part Two

The forms of writing

10.

Description

Successful description makes the reader see, hear, smell, taste, or feel, as the particular situation demands. It presents its subject—an Arabian camel driver, a Los Angeles intersection, an autumn scene, or whatever else—so that the reader can perceive that subject clearly.

In the passages presented below, note how each writer is attempting to make you see, hear, and feel what he sees, hears, and feels.

- Now Henry dresses shabbily and has let his hair grow long. He carries a heavy cane and as he goes through the streets of the town boys crow at him. They imitate the cackle of hens that have been at the business of laying eggs and the clarion cry of the rooster. Henry grows violently angry. He waves his cane about, he swears, he pursues the boys furiously but never catches them. As he passes through Main Street some man, standing in a group of men by the post office, also crows. Henry approaches the group. His hands are trembling. He stands before them demanding justice.   [Sherwood Anderson, "Small Town People," 1940.]

- There was a light mask of snow on the fields, and the air was smoky: the whole earth seemed to smoke and steam, and from the windows of the train one could see the wet earth and the striped cultivated pattern of the fields, and now and then some farm buildings. It did not look like America: the land looked fat and well kept, and even the smoky wintry woods had this well-kept appearance. Far off sometimes one could see tall lines of poplars and knew that there was water there. [Thomas Wolfe, "The Sun and the Rain," 1934.]

Clarity of expression takes precedence over all else in descriptive writing. The writer must describe every item so clearly that the reader can see the subject completely on the first reading. Good descriptive writing can have no haze, no shadows, no blurring film between reader and subject. The two passages below are characterized by the requisite clarity of expression.

● It was market-day, and over all the roads round Goderville, the peasants and their wives were coming towards the town. The men walked easily, lurching the whole body forward at every step. Their long legs were twisted and deformed by the slow, painful labors of the country: —by bending over to plough, which is what also makes their shoulders too high and their figures crooked; and by reaping corn, which obliges them for steadiness' sake to spread their knees too wide. Their starched blue blouses, shining as though varnished, ornamented at collar and cuffs with little patterns of white stitchwork, and blown up big around their bony bodies, seemed exactly like balloons about to soar, but putting forth a head, two arms, and two feet. [Guy de Maupassant, "A Piece of String," 1928.]

● The skyline of the city of London in 1973 is very different from what it was when, exactly two hundred and fifty years ago, the body of Sir Christopher Wren was carried to its simple tomb beneath the dome of St. Paul's. It is even very different from what it was in the late forties when the undecorated boredom of modern "vertical features" in ferro-concrete first began to challenge Wren's cathedral and his surviving City churches. Today, new pedestrian precincts girdle a renovated St. Paul's; there is a new London Bridge under construction; the complex of new urban tower blocks approaches completion; and at last most of the Wren architecture that survived the second Great Fire of London is ably and respectfully restored. This is, therefore, an appropriate moment to reassess the life and work

of the man whose elegant variety of invention still holds pride
of place amid so much undistinguished anonymity. What
manner of man was Wren, what was his background and what
was his life's work?   [Harold F. Hutchison, "Sir Christopher
Wren," *History Today*, April 1973.]

A second attribute of effective descriptive writing is fidelity to
actual fact. The reader must feel certain of the writer's honesty, or
conversely, of the writer's aversion to any kind of exaggeration or
distortion.

Unlike the standard real estate sales advertisement or the
chamber of commerce brochure that pictures its city as another
Versailles, good description tells the truth. There is no deception, no
half truth. There is only a constant and forthright attempt to be
accurate.

The two selections below describe widely different subjects.
They have in common, however, the honesty of presentation that
sound description must possess.

● The *Mother Feeding Her Child* is another interesting work. This
  is a smaller but still heavy carving of a different kind of wood,
  hard but light brown in color. The carving is rough: the chisel
  marks are clearly evident, the imperfections have been retained
  or modified, the termite damage left for all to see. Omari has
  used the universal symbol of mother and child to show the
  people of a particular tribe defending and protecting its cultural
  and social traditions. The masses of the figure are heavy, bulky,
  perhaps immovable; the carving of the features and details are
  angular and rudimentary; the torso and mother's head are far
  too large for the squatting legs. But tenderness is conveyed.
     There were several other large carvings in the exhibition
  including one, the largest and nine feet high, titled *Climbing
  Figures*. This kind of carving may be thought of as the artist's
  skill in using the changes of direction, imperfections and general
  character of the wood.   [Donald Bowen, "Exhibitions at the
  Commonwealth Institute," *African Arts*, Winter 1973.]

● I have seen the same dark forest plantations in the Scottish
  Highlands, relieved only by occasional woodlands, harboring

broad-leaved trees, at the lower elevations or in village streets. The multicolored leaves were falling into the creeks, russet and yellows drifting towards the sea. It made one wish he could have seen this part of Britain with its heather-clad mountains and pellucid lakes when it was clothed with deciduous trees, standing in forests as far as the eye could see.

Although there is strong control of rural land-use in Britain, forestry has been exempted from such restrictions except where amenity interests brought the foresters to a bargaining table. For example, in the Chiltern hills, where the spreading beech woods are the glory of the landscape, the Forestry Commission, county councils and private landowners (who usually own vast estates) "are moving towards a voluntary arrangement to control felling cycles," says the Commission, "and to ensure a continuing broad-leaved landscape." This amounts to an admission, says the Ramblers' Association, that "conifers are alien and unsightly in outstanding landscapes." [Anthony Netboy, "British Forestry and Its Problems," *American Forests*, January 1973.]

A third attribute of effective description is overall interest or appeal. Ideally, a reader should be drawn to a descriptive passage as he is drawn to the rail of the ship entering an old world harbor or as he is attracted to a group of foreign visitors in native garb at the United Nations building.

There is no formula for establishing such appeal. Yet by looking hard at the subject to be described, you can find the qualities that first attracted you. You should then strive to describe these qualities in a manner that will create the same attraction for your readers.

Study the two passages presented below. What makes these descriptions appealing to you, the reader?

● There was another helpless silence at the table. Joe sprawled uneasily in his seat, not willing to go till the family conclave was dissolved. Fred Henry, the second brother, was erect, clean-limbed, alert. He had watched the passing of the horses with more sang-froid. If he was an animal, like Joe, he was an animal which controls, not one which is controlled. He was master of any horse, and he carried himself with a well-tempered air of mastery. But he was not master of the situations of life. He pushed his coarse brown moustache upwards, off his lip, and glanced irritably at his sister, who sat impassive and inscrutable. [D. H. Lawrence, "The Horse Dealer's Daughter," 1922.]

● Now, the old priest inside the confessional was a very aged man. He was so old and feeble that the community rarely allowed him to do anything but say Mass and hear Confessions. Whenever they let him preach he would ramble on and on for an hour; people would get up and go away; the sacristan would peep out in despair through the sacristy door; and in the end an altar-boy would be sent out to ring the great gong on the altar-steps to make him stop. I have seen the boy come out three times to the gong before the old man could be lured down from the pulpit.   [Sean O'Faolain, "Innocence," 1948.]

11.

Narration

Narration details in proper order the incidents that constitute an event or occurrence. It tells the reader exactly what happened so that he can understand the full nature of the event or occurrence. For example, when you write about an automobile accident, you present, in order, all the incidents within the total event—the accident. Your aim is to make your reader understand just how and why the accident occurred. To do this, describe the direction in which the cars were moving, their rate of speed, the physical impact, and all other facts necessary for a complete account. Meanwhile, you strive throughout to make your reader comprehend the cause, character, and results of the accident.

Note how, in the selection below, the author has included all necessary explanation for a series of incidents.

- One evening not too long ago, Nelson Wright (Dick) Freeman, 64-year-old chairman of Tenneco Inc., was walking alone on New York's Park Avenue heading for a quiet supper. Up came a junkie. Freeman, from relatively placid Houston, kept walking. The junkie flashed a knife and snarled, "I'm going to slit your goddamned throat."

  No help was nearby, so Freeman replied, "We'd better visit headquarters first," and drew from his right hip pocket a metal clasp enscribed "Harris County Deputy Sheriff." Harris, of course, is just a Texas county, but the junkie fled and left

Freeman walking calmly toward his supper.   ["An Embarrass-
ment of Projects," *Forbes*, April 15, 1973.]

Narration most commonly presents incidents in chronological
order, but when it is used to convey a motive, purpose, or
explanation, the writer often subordinates the natural time pattern
to other considerations. For instance, he may state one or two
conclusions and then select incidents to substantiate those conclusions.

Note how the writer of the selection below has used the
narrative element as a basis for explaining her main concern: the
cause of a specific patient's headaches.

● John, a good-natured businessman, apparently happily married
for five years, suffered from diffuse inhibitions and "inferiority
feelings" and in recent years had developed occasional headaches without any detectable physical basis. He had not been
analyzed but he was fairly familiar with the psychoanalytic way
of thinking. Later he came to me for analysis of a rather
intricate character neurosis, and his experience in working alone
was one of the factors that convinced him of the possible value
of psychoanalytic therapy.

When he started to analyze his headaches it was without
intending to do so. He, his wife, and two friends went to a
musical comedy and he developed a headache during the play.
This struck him as queer because he had felt well before going
to the theatre. At first, with some irritation, he ascribed his
headache to the fact that the play was bad and the evening was
a waste of time, but he soon realized that after all one does not
get headaches from a bad play. Now that he thought about it,
the play was not so bad after all. But of course it was nothing
compared with the play of Shaw's that he would have preferred.
These last words stuck in his mind—he "would have preferred."
Here he felt a flash of anger and saw the connection. He had
been overruled when the choice between the plays was up for
discussion. It was not even much of a discussion: he felt he
should be a good sport, and what did it matter anyhow.
Apparently it had mattered to him, however, and he had been
deeply angry about being coerced. With that recognition the

headache was gone. He realized also that this was not the first headache that originated in this way. There were bridge parties, for instance, which he hated to join but was persuaded to do so.   [Karen Horney, *Self-Analysis*, 1942.]

Narration is not limited to literary endeavors. It is, in fact, one of the most common types of writing done in the workaday world. For example, the police official's report on how a clash erupted between strikers and nonstrikers at a local mill is narrative writing. The writer presents the background; then he traces out the successive incidents leading to the clash.

Similarly, a case history of any kind is largely narrative. The social service worker outlines a family history; the physician details the development of a patient's disease; the elementary school teacher writes a report on class progress during the school year; the sales manager explains how sales fell off in a specific area over a five-year period. Each is engaged in narrative writing.

Below is an official entry from the record book of a local volunteer fire company. Note the narrative structure.

●   September 21, 1973

Today at 2:21 p.m., this company responded to a telephone call from Harmon J. Latrobe, 221 N. Weston St., Frazier Township, who informed us that a small garage at the rear of his home was on fire.

This company, directed by Lt. Wm. H. Jeremy, arrived at the scene of the fire at approximately 2:31 p.m. We found that the building, a one-car garage made of brick with wooden doors and roof, was burning badly from within.

We hooked our main line to a hydrant just across the street and brought the fire under control at approximately 2:45 p.m.

The cause of the fire was a painter's blow torch which Mr. Latrobe had left burning when he went to answer a telephone call in his home. He was preparing the torch to use in removing paint from the side of his house, which he was to paint.

Mr. Latrobe estimates the damage at approximately $1,800.

The roof of the garage is completely destroyed. The wooden doors of the garage are completely destroyed. A wooden work bench and some other small items are completely destroyed.

This company left the scene of the fire at 3:10 p.m., after checking to make certain that all fire had been completely extinguished.

> Vincent G. Burns
> First Sergeant
> Company #2

Before you can produce acceptable narrative writing, you must know the essential qualities involved. Above all else, you must have an appealing fluency; that is, your writing must flow easily and naturally, enabling your reader to follow without strain or puzzlement. Your expression, like a well constructed road, must carry your reader along without discomforting effects. Or stated in other terms, your reader must always feel relaxed and comfortable. Note, for instance, how easily you can follow the passage below because of the general clarity of expression, the logical placement of detail, and the overall ease of movement.

- Thrown out of work, Lewiston drifted aimlessly about Chicago, from pillar to post, working a little, earning here a dollar, there a dime, but always sinking, sinking, till at last the ooze of the lowest bottom dragged at his feet and the rush of the great ebb went over him and engulfed him and shut him out from the light, and a park bench became his home and the "bread line" his chief makeshift of subsistence.

  He stood now in the enfolding drizzle, sodden, stupefied with fatigue. Before and behind stretched the line. There was no talking. There was no sound. The street was empty. It was so still that the passing of a cable-car in the adjoining thoroughfare grated like prolonged rolling explosions, beginning and ending at immeasurable distances. The drizzle descended incessantly. After a long time midnight struck. . . .

  The period of waiting on this night of rain seemed endless to those silent, hungry men; but at length there was a stir. The line moved. The side door opened. Ah, at last! They were going to hand out the bread.

  But instead of the usual white aproned undercook with his crowded hampers there now appeared in the doorway a new man—a young fellow who looked like a bookkeeper's assistant. He bore in his hand a placard, which he tacked to the outside of the door. Then he disappeared within the bakery, locking the door after him.

A shudder of poignant despair, an unformed inarticulate sense of calamity, seemed to run from end to end of the line. What had happened? Those in the rear, unable to read the placard, surged forward, a sense of bitter disappointment clutching at their hearts.

The line broke up, disintegrated into a shapeless throng—a throng that crowded forward and collected in front of the shut door whereon the placard was affixed. Lewiston, with the others, pushed forward. On the placard he read these words:

"Owing to the fact that the price of grain has been increased to two dollars a bushel, there will be no distribution of bread from this bakery until further notice."   [Frank Norris, "A Deal in Wheat," 1901.]

The following passage should help you appreciate the importance of fluency. You have to fight your way through it because of the clumsy sentence structure, the vague phraseology, and the general looseness of the structure. The writer is an eighteen-year-old boy. What advice would you give him to improve his work?

○ Last night when my brother came in, my youngest brother, he had a big white rabbit that he had bought at one of the stations at the farmer's market at the other end of town. I don't know what he thought he was going to do with the thing, but he had bought it, and I guess that he planned to keep it. He is really hard to understand sometimes. You never know what he will do next. I mean you can never really know.

Well, he had the rabbit, and when my father began to ask questions about the plans for the rabbit and his future, he was a bit puzzled. The whole conversation between the two of them began to get bogged down in some sort of argument or exchange of differing opinions about where the rabbit was to be kept. Who was to feed him, and who was to be the major domo of the whole business.

The argument was never really settled. My brother put the rabbit down on the floor, and he began to sniff a bit, but that is all he did.

In addition to fluency, sound narrative writing is characterized by the presence of all pertinent detail. Narration that leaves questions unanswered, treats its subject superficially, or creates an aura of unfinished business is unacceptable.

After you finish reading the selection below, you sense that the author has included every necessary point.

● At General Motors' Flint, Michigan, Fisher Body Number One, the largest auto-body factory in the world, it was early evening of a chill winter day. Suddenly a bright red light began flashing in the window of the United Automobile Workers union hall across the street from the plant's main gate. It was the signal for an emergency union meeting.

When the swing shift took its dinner break at 8:00 P.M., excited workers crowded into the hall. UAW organizer Robert C. Travis confirmed the rumor crackling through the huge plant: dies for the presses that stamped out car body panels were being loaded into freight cars on a Fisher One spur track. Two days earlier, he reminded the men, fellow unionists had struck the Fisher Body plant in Cleveland; now, fearing Flint would be next, General Motors was trying to transfer the vital stamping dies to its other plants. "Well, what are we going to do about it?" Travis asked.

"Well, them's our jobs," a man said. "We want them left right here in Flint." There was a chorus of agreement. "What do you want to do?" Travis asked.

"Shut her down! Shut the goddam plant!" In a moment the hall was a bedlam of cheering.

As the dinner break ended, the men streamed back into Fisher One. Travis was watching anxiously in front of the union hall when the starting whistle blew. Instead of the usual answering pound of machinery, there was only silence. For long minutes nothing seemed to be happening. Then a third-floor window swung open and a worker leaned out, waving exultantly to Travis. "She's ours!" he shouted.

Thus began, on December 30, 1936, the great Flint sit-down strike, the most momentous confrontation between American labor and management in this century. For the next six weeks Flint would be a lead story in newspapers, newsreels, and radio newscasts. Events there dramatized the new militancy of the American worker, a mass movement that was to produce basic changes in the relationship of capital and labor. To those in sympathy with labor's goal of unionizing the auto industry, the rambunctious young United Automobile Workers union was David challenging the General Motors Goliath. To those dedicated to the sanctity of property, the UAW and its methods posed a radical, revolutionary threat to industrial capitalism. Few observers were neutral about the Flint sit-down.   [Stephen W. Sears, "Shut the Goddam Plant," *American Heritage*, April/May 1982.]

A third attribute of effective narration is interest. You must be able to create a curiosity in the reader and then reward that curiosity. In the hands of the right writer, any subject can be made "downright" interesting to the vast majority of readers. Therefore, you must learn to be the *right* writer for your subject.

Note the interest that emanates from the selection presented below. Its author could have written a dry legal brief; instead, he has produced exciting narrative.

● Jim Noerr downed his morning tea and headed out across the barnyard, unaware of the tragedy that awaited him. In the barn, dark and hushed like an empty church, he began to sing. Noerr likes to sing—or used to—and anyway it was almost Christmas, 1962.

Bending his six-foot-four frame under a low beam he opened the door to the leafing shed and the cows barged through to their stanchions. All but one.

She stood outside on unsteady legs, her head swaying eerily back and forth. Finally she veered drunkenly into the cement alleyway. Noerr watched in horror as the hapless animal fell to her side and began to pound her head against the floor with sickening dull blows. He raced for the phone.

"Sounds like some form of poisoning," his vet told him. Mercifully, the cow was dead before Noerr got back to the barn.

By the end of January, three more cows had died, and the whole herd was sick. Noerr trucked two of the three carcasses to Pennsylvania State University, 35 miles from his farm in Mifflin County. Vets and lab technicians suspected lead poisoning, but evidence was not positively established until 1963.

No source of the poisoning could be found. Dr. Sam Guss, of Penn State, visited the farm. He could locate no source of contamination either. Puzzled, he stood in the barnyard and gazed down the road.

"What's all that smoke down there?" he asked.

"That's a smelting plant," Noerr explained. "They reclaim brass and lead from scrap metal."

"Does that smoke ever hang low over your fields?"

"Yes. Sometimes it's terrible."

The two men looked at each other. Could it be—that lead fall-out from the smoke had settled on the ground or crops and the cows ate it?

The circumstantial evidence was there but could Noerr prove it? "We tried to keep on farming for a while," he recounts, "but it seemed hopeless. Every time I tried to use my own feed, the cows got sicker. When I bought feed, they seemed to get better, but I couldn't afford to buy all my feed."

Production fell; analysis of forage showed unusual lead content. Extension specialists felt the evidence pointed to the smelter. "I tried to talk to the plant owners, but couldn't convince them the smelter was at fault," says Noerr. So he sued. . . .

Judge Paul S. Lehman, in a 61 page opinion, ruled against Sitkin, awarding the Noerrs $52,360.30, arrived at by computing all losses of cattle and production income by year with interest compounded. [Gene Logsdon, "He Tackled a Giant and Won," *Farm Journal*, May 1973.]

A fourth attribute of good narrative writing is the reflection of a pleasing personality. The writer must be authoritative but not patronizing, assertive but not dogmatic, enthusiastic but not gushy. In essence, his personality must blend attractively into the particular task before him.

A Washington Irving succeeds, among other things, because of the charm of his humor, a Sherwood Anderson because of his wholesome solicitousness for his fellow human beings, and a Norman Mailer because of his empathy with the normal person's inability to comprehend the complex society in which he lives.

Although the element of personality is stronger in some narrative writing than in others, remember that every time you write, your personality is on display.

Examine the passage below. What kind of personality does it reflect?

- And when Dora came to talk to him [in jail] the next morning at nine o'clock, his alarm proved to be well-founded. Dora was cold, detached, deliberate. She was not at all what he had hoped she might be—sympathetic and helpful. She didn't volunteer to get a lawyer, or in fact to do anything—and when she listened quietly to his story, it seemed to him that she had the appearance of a person listening to a very improbable lie. Again, as he narrated the perfectly simple episode—the discussion of "impulse" at the bridge game, the drinks, and the absurd tipsy desire to try a harmless little experiment—again, as when he talked to the store detective, he heard his own voice becoming hollow and insincere. It was exactly as if he knew himself to be guilty. His throat grew dry, he began to falter, to lose his thread, to use the wrong words. When he stopped speaking finally, Dora was silent.

  "Well, say something!" he said angrily, after a moment. "Don't just stare at me. I'm not a criminal."

  "I'll get a lawyer for you," she answered, "but that's all I can do."

  "Look here, Dora—you don't mean you—"

  He looked at her incredulously. It wasn't possible that she really thought him a thief? And suddenly, as he looked at her, he realized how long it was since he had really known this woman. They had drifted apart. She was embittered, that was it—embittered by his non-success.   [Conrad Aiken, "Impulse," 1950.]

After you have learned thoroughly the previously discussed attributes of narration, you are ready for one final concept. Sometimes narration is so closely related to exposition that it must be termed "expository narration." This type of narration is used, for example, by the botanist explaining the life cycle of the plant, by the oceanographer explaining the movement of tides, and by the pilot explaining the handling of an airplane.

The purpose of the selection below is to explain (exposition). To do this, the author relates the story of how a particular town became a fish-catching and fish-processing center (narration). Hence his work is expository narration.

- The beautifully sheltered cove on the northern tip of the island of Heimaey has been of considerable importance to Iceland's development. There is no satisfactory harbour anywhere along the 400 kilometres of outwash sands that make up the south coast of Iceland itself, and Heimaey is now the main fish-catching and fish-processing centre of southern Iceland. It reaps the generous harvest of the adjacent sea bed.

  When catches and dividends multiplied with the advent of steam-powered boats after 1906, people streamed to the island until, by 1929, the harbour housed 100 fishing boats and the town had expanded across the low lava ramp north of Helgafell. Catches by line and net provided the basis for the rise of fish-processing and related industries, and led to the establishment of ice plants, fish meal plants, liver processors, net makers, fish marketing companies, workshops, ship-building yards and all kinds of services. There was a serious slump in the 1930s but a post World War II revival has proceeded in leaps and bounds to the present day.   [Chalmers M. Clapperton, "Thrice Threatened Heimaey," *Geographical Magazine*, April 1973.]

12.

Exposition

Exposition is writing designed to explain. It is writing that seeks to elucidate the basic nature of a specific condition, situation, process, viewpoint, or similar matter. A report on wildlife in the mountains of Tennessee, a textbook on political science, a judge's written opinion in a court case, and a chemist's account of the effects of chlorine on the human epidermis are all examples of expository writing. In each case, the central purpose of the writing is explanation.

As you compose your work, your primary fidelity must always be to actual fact. You must present the subject exactly as it exists—without embellishment, distortion, or other misrepresentations of significant detail. In explaining the physical character of an urban area, for example, you must strive for absolutely objective treatment of the subject. You must discuss accurately the impressive suburban sections with their custom-built homes, their carefully tended lawns, and their tree-lined streets, and you must describe with equal candor the run-down neighborhoods, the dirty streets of the tenement districts, and the graffiti-marked store fronts in some areas where teenagers congregate. Furthermore, you must not allow your personal opinions to obscure or color the facts.

In the paragraph below, the author has met the requirements of fidelity to actual fact. As she explains the character of a small town, she selects her detail and presents her findings without praising or disparaging her subject.

- It is a town not wholly without traditions. Residents will point out the two-hundred-year-old manor house, now a minor museum; and in the autumn they line the streets on a scheduled evening to watch the Volunteer Firemen parade. That is a fine occasion, with so many heads of households marching in their red blouses and white gloves, some with flaming helmets, some swinging lanterns, most of them genially out of step. There is a bigger parade on Memorial Day with more marchers than watchers and with the Catholic priest, the rabbi, and the Protestant ministers each delivering a short prayer when the paraders gather near the War Memorial. On the whole, however, outside of contributing generously to the Community Chest, Manorites are not addicted to municipal get-togethers. [Phyllis McGinley, *A Short Walk From the Station*, 1962.]

A second attribute of sound expository writing is *completeness*. The reader must be satisfied that he has seen a total picture, that nothing has been concealed or suppressed. However, because writers cannot always include every detail they must make a judicious selection from the evidence available. In writing of urban population shifts, for instance, the writer would probably find at least twenty reasons why people move. As a result, he would have to assess these reasons and select the major ones for extensive discussion while only mentioning others in passing.

Note in the selection below the author's ability to capture in a single paragraph the qualities, conditions, and atmosphere that characterize the jungle night.

- The tropical jungle by day is the most wonderful place in the world. At night I am sure it is the most weirdly beautiful of all places outside the world. For it is primarily unearthly, unreal; and at last I came to know why. In the light of the full moon it was rejuvenated. The simile of theatrical scenery was always present to the mind, the illusion lying especially in the completeness of transformation from the jungle by daylight. The theatrical effect was heightened by the sense of being in some vast building. This was due to the complete absence of any breath of air. Not a leaf moved; even the pendulous air-roots reaching down their seventy-foot plummets for the touch of soil did not sway a hair's breadth. The throb of the pulse set the rhythm for one's steps. The silence, for a time, was as perfect as the breathlessness. It was a wonderfully ventilated amphitheatre; the air was as free from any feeling of tropical heat, as it lacked all crispness of the north. It was exactly the temperature of one's skin. Heat and cold were for the moment as unthinkable as wind.   [William Beebe, *Jungle Peace*, 1918.]

A third attribute of sound expository writing is a pleasing note of *authority*. Even when treating a personal viewpoint, the writer must convey the impression of having considered his material in a calm, thorough, capable manner.

The note of authority emanates from the tone of the writing rather than from anything the writer claims by direct statement. The reader senses the writer's confidence is based on knowledge of a subject genuinely understood.

In the selection below, a businessman-turned-political-office-holder has taken a complex subject—the need for the federal government to plan its future operations—and has explained convincingly many of its aspects. He leaves the impression that he has reflected on his subject capably and thoroughly.

● If we are to manage the future, we must do something any large bureaucracy finds painful: inventing the questions before we start providing the answers, being careful, of course, that they are the relevant, new questions and not the obsolete, if comfortable, old ones. It is sad but true that old questions rarely die or even fade away.

There is also the critical question of priorities in managing the future. I notice some important differences between the way the government approaches the balance between short-term needs and long-term planning, and the way that many of our best managed business enterprises do. The effective corporate manager, like the effective politician, understands that if he doesn't meet yesterday's commitments today, he may not be around to see, and hopefully enjoy, whether he will attain today's goals tomorrow. That is why the efforts to improve program management, to improve current operations, are absolutely necessary.

But to say they are necessary is not to say they are sufficient. One yardstick I found useful in assessing the real strength of a company was how much time its very best people devoted to the future. Wherever I saw most or all of a company pre-occupied with today's and next month's and even this year's problems, very frequently I found an enterprise either already or going to be in trouble, unprepared to meet either the adversities or the opportunities of tomorrow. This, of course, is important since a corporation, like a government, is an institution chartered in perpetuity and not just for today.

Using this criterion, many of today's best managed corporations invest substantial amounts of their most precious resources—their time—on the future: projecting the future, defining the problems and the opportunities, and deciding how to best shape the future instead of being shocked by it.

Men at the top of our governmental structure find themselves enmeshed in a system which almost seems to have been designed to prevent such thought. Consider for a few moments the barriers to a futuristic orientation. The President and all other political executives constantly face an election that looms no more than four years ahead. Elections pressure all political actors to reduce their time horizon. The future which most concerns them is the time between now and the next election. To lose power is to lose the chance to do anything. Likewise, the multiple roles performed by the President and cabinet members reduce the time available for thinking about more than the most immediate tomorrows. Additionally, the men at the top of our government find large amounts of time consumed by ceremonial duties, speech-making, and politicking. None of these things are bad, many are fun, but they all take time.   [Peter G. Peterson, "The Challenge of Managing the Future," *Good Government*, Summer 1972.]

A fourth attribute of sound expository writing is one that has been stressed repeatedly throughout this book—*clarity*. Every sentence must be so cast that it presents its thoughts lucidly on the first reading. Never should the reader be forced to untangle involved sentence structures, to ponder over the meaning of an ambiguous statement, or to struggle with vague or hazy phraseology. The writer must present every thought so forthrightly and pointedly that it carries the reader along comfortably and with understanding. In other words, well-written exposition should be so phrased that any competent reader can follow it without question or perplexity.

Examine the selection below. Although sometimes scored as lacking in sound critical judgment, it is nonetheless characterized by genuine clarity of expression. The author has certainly explained his conclusions in clear, unmistakable terms.

- Mr. Howells was one of the gentlest, sweetest, and most honest of men, but he had the code of a pious old maid whose greatest delight was to have tea at the vicarage. He abhorred not only profanity and obscenity but all of what H. G. Wells has called "the jolly coarseness of life." In his fantastic vision of life, which he innocently conceived to be realistic, farmers and seamen and factory-hands might exist, but the farmer must never be covered with muck, the seaman must never roll out bawdy chanteys, the factory-hand must be thankful to his good kind employer, and all of them must long for the opportunity to visit Florence and smile gently at the quaintness of the beggars.

  So strongly did Howells feel this genteel, this New Humanistic philosophy that he was able vastly to influence his contemporaries, down even to 1914 and the turmoil of the Great War.

  He was actually able to tame Mark Twain, perhaps the greatest of our writers, and to put that fiery old savage into an intellectual frock coat and top hat. His influence is not altogether gone today. He is still worshipped by Hamlin Garland, an author who should in every way have been greater than Howells but who under Howells' influence was changed from a harsh and magnificent realist into a genial and insignificant lecturer. Mr. Garland is, so far as we have one, the dean of American letters today, and as our dean, he is alarmed by all the younger writers who are so lacking in taste as to suggest that men and women do not always love in accordance with the prayer-book, and that common people sometimes use language which would be inappropriate at a women's literary club on Main Street. Yet this same Hamlin Garland, as a young man, before he had gone to Boston and become cultured and

Howellsised, wrote two most valiant and revelatory works of realism, "Main Travelled Roads" and "Rose of Dutcher's Colly." [Sinclair Lewis, Nobel Prize address, 1930.]

There are five commonly accepted classifications of exposition: definition, analysis, clarification, comparison, and explanation of relationships.

Definition

Whenever a subject is unusually complex, the writer may find it best to explain it by presenting a series of definitions. By isolating the main parts of the subject and then defining each part thoroughly, the writer explains the total subject.

For instance, an economist seeking to explain recessions will compose an exhaustive definition of a recession by isolating its primary characteristics: decline in the gross national product, increase in unemployment, and general sluggishness of the economy. After demonstrating that these characteristics must be recognized in any satisfactory explanation of a recession, the economist defines each one—thereby constructing a definition, hence an explanation, of recession.

Explaining by defining is not always a simple matter. Some subjects—intelligence quotients or cellular growth within the human body, for example—may contain so many subtleties and controversial aspects that explaining them by definition can be quite challenging. Yet in these and similar instances, exposition by definition is the best means of making the subject clear.

The following selection illustrates the process of exposition by definition.

● Let me begin by stripping off the theoretical trappings and frills from the marketplace concept and looking at business in the simplest way possible.

A market is the place where the links that hold business affairs together are made. A link is a transaction, typically involving two independent parties, each of which has a number of competitors. Every transaction is a *single* sales-purchase decision mutually arrived at, through bargaining, by the two parties that have chosen to enter into a commitment, a contract, or some other kind of a bilateral agreement with each other.

Bargaining and competition are thus complementary stages, or aspects, or methods, of reaching the decision to transact, but they are quite distinct:

Bargaining is negotiating, comparing, making choices, and arriving at an agreement with a partner—a supplier or a customer—who himself has been negotiating, comparing, and making choices. The bargaining relationship is characterized by a direct buyer-seller relationship across the counter or trading table; and the keynote of this relationship is *making choices among the available options*. Both parties make such choices as they barter.

Competition refers to all those who come into the market-place with similar wares to offer. It refers, that is, to a group, standing on one side of the market, each of whose members *seeks to be chosen*, by a prospective partner from the other side of the market, at the expense of his fellows.

Put another way, a competitor, whether he is a buyer or a seller, seeks to be chosen by a potential partner with whom he can bargain; whereas a bargainer trades options back and forth with his bargaining partner until the two of them have written a mutually acceptable agreement (or, possibly, reached a stalemate). Bargainers make decisions among choices and options; competitors seek to be chosen.

This same difference between bargaining and competition is reflected in two familiar rules of business strategy: "Don't bargain with the competition" and "Don't compete with your best customer."

Now, it is extraordinary, but true, that although the two concepts are distinct, they have grown together into a single, amorphous entity in most people's minds. Perhaps this is because we have relied so very strongly on competition ("seeking to be chosen") and bargaining ("choice making among alternatives") working *together*, working *jointly*. In tandem, the two have made such an excellent team that we now fail to recognize the fact that each one makes a distinct contribution. [Henry B. Arthur, "On Rivalry in the Marketplace," *Harvard Business Review*, September/October 1972.]

Analysis

Exposition by analysis is simply the separation of a subject into logical or natural divisions, the thorough examination of each division, and the explanation of its nature.

The process of exposition by analysis is commonly undertaken by persons in all walks of life. The President of the United States explaining the state of the nation's economy to his television audience, the salesman explaining the mechanism of a vacuum cleaner, the sports commentator explaining the trick play—all are separating their subjects into their component parts and then analyzing each part.

The first requirement of exposition by analysis is the ability to divide a subject logically into clearly discernible sections. In treating physical objects, the process can be quite simple.

The garden equipment salesman, for instance, can explain a new lawn mower easily by separating his total subject into discussions of the motor, the cutting equipment, the accelerator, and other components. Similarly, the ski slope director can give the newcomer a clear picture of how to ski on the particular slope by explaining the run itself, the use of the starting area, the operation of the chair lift, and so forth.

When you are handling abstract ideas, the process is more challenging. The political scientist, for example, often meets involved problems in trying to elucidate the philosophy of a political party. Separating the philosophy into major and minor parts is anything but simple.

The following selection is an example of exposition by analysis. Notice especially the approach employed in dividing the subject into parts and the success of the subsequent analysis.

● Bulbs are really for beginners. A bulb is something of a miracle—leaves, stems and flowers, all compacted into one highly efficient storehouse. It has only to be planted in the proper season and undergo a suitable period of time at suitable temperatures, and there is hardly anything short of accident or malicious mishandling that can keep it from producing flowers.

It almost takes more energy and talent to *keep a bulb from flowering* than to produce prize blooms, and that is why bulbs are so ideally suited for the first venture into gardening. On top of that, many of the hardy bulbs are so durable that they come up year after year after year. Daffodils, crocuses, snowdrops, grape hyacinths not only persist, but multiply.

With all this obliging performance and insurance of success it is always surprising to find how few new gardeners have caught on to using bulbs, and how much misunderstanding still exists about how and why they do perform so well.

A bulb is in one sense a whole plant in more or less dormant state, magnificently packed into a neat, durable, easy-to-handle structure. In autumn a single tulip bulb contains in reduced state the leaves, stem and flower parts, and enough stored carbohydrate—the largest portion of the bulb—to nourish the plant and insure its viability. Even while a tulip bulb is out of the ground and seemingly in a dormant state metabolism continues and the flower, stem and leaves develop, however inconspicuously, within the bulb, provided storage temperatures are correct. If you cut a tulip bulb open carefully in November you can find and separate leaf and flower tissue, and these parts are larger than they were in September. It is well to remember, dormant though they appear, that bulbs are living (organic) entities and, as such, are due respectful treatment.

Knowing that the bulb is largely a food storehouse to sustain the embryo-like plant, it is easier to understand why, after a bulb has flowered, it is necessary for the leaves to continue to function for as long as possible. Green leaves are food factories. Tulip and daffodil and crocus leaves manufacture food and store it in the new bulb (or bulb-like structure) in order to nourish the next year's flower. By the same token the practice of removing the old flower, so that seed production is prevented, insures that all of the carbohydrate produced goes into the bulb and not into seeds, which are also food storehouses. Growers of prize daffodils, for instance, are so aware of the food-producing function of the green parts of their plants that they are very careful to remove only the old flower, leaving the flower stem which is green and which functions like a leaf in the photosynthetic process. More green tissue means more photosynthesis and more carbohydrate production.

Perhaps bulbs are the original recyclers; they are, at least, a very wonderful and easy-to-see example of growth, flowering and replenishment. They are not only good subjects for beginning gardeners but a joy and a lesson for all.   [Carlton B. Lees, Editorial, *Horticulture*, October 1972.]

Clarification

Exposition by clarification is especially useful when a subject is either widely misunderstood or likely to be misunderstood. In such instances, this approach gives the writer a natural springboard from which to explain a topic as well as an opportunity to generate reader interest by correcting a popular misconception.

In the writing presented below, the authors explain one of America's most familiar birds by clarifying common misconceptions. Note how this approach generates interest in the subject.

● On every vernal morning a wave of Robin song rises on the Atlantic coast to hail the coming day, and so, preceding the rising sun, rolls across the land until at last it breaks and dies away upon the distant shores of the Pacific Ocean. All through the Northern States the Robin ushers in the day with song. Hot or cold, wet or dry, the Robin sings. He makes himself at home in the back yard; he hops about on the lawn; he knows all the folks and they all know him. Why then should one write about his haunts and habits, which should be well known to everybody? In answer to this it may be said in truth that most people really know very little about him.

To begin with he is not a robin and never was one. The real "Robin Redbreast" is a native of the Old World—a little bird formed much like our Eastern Bluebird with a dark brown back and a reddish-orange throat and breast. This is the "Robin" that appears so often in European literature and folklore—the one that covered with leaves the "Babes in the Wood." Our so-called Robin is a large migratory thrush with a reddish-brown or tawny breast, but our forefathers named him Robin in remembrance of the beloved English bird and despite the protests of naturalists the name sticks.

Another thing about this bird that most people do not know is that many Robins spend the entire winter in the latitude of New England, where they roost among the evergreens in swamps, feed on winter berries and come out into the fields occasionally when the snow has vanished during a thaw. This common habit is so little known that nearly every winter the newspapers publish articles predicting an early spring because the "first Robin" has appeared or because "the Robins have arrived early." In some winters when persistent berries are abundant in the North hundreds of Robins pass the winter in New Brunswick and Nova Scotia, but this is unusual. Most of our Robins, however, go south in winter and probably all those that winter in the Northern States are hardy birds that nest in Ungava or Labrador, and even some of these perish of privation and cold in severe winters. . . .

Apparently the northward movement of Robins begins before spring opens. Not infrequently Robins appear in considerable numbers in January. Large flocks have been seen at that season in Maine and many in Nova Scotia, but we cannot assume that such birds are on their way north. More likely they are late migrants from the interior; but in late February and early March there is evident some northward movement. [Edward Howe Forbush and John Bichard, *A Natural History of American Birds*, 1955.]

Comparison

Exposition by comparison is based on the concept that to explain any unfamiliar object or idea, you must compare it with an object or idea familiar to the reader.

Exposition by comparison is especially useful in explaining such subjects as a *particular* Oriental people, a *given* car's performance, and a red shouldered hawk's flight. In each instance, you proceed by making appropriate comparisons and contrasts.

Below is a sound example of exposition by comparison.

● I have long had an image in my mind of what constitutes

liberty. Suppose that I were building a great piece of powerful machinery, and suppose that I should so awkwardly and unskillfully assemble the parts of it that every time one part tried to move it would be interfered with by the others, and the whole thing would buckle up and be checked. Liberty for the several parts would consist in the best possible assembling and adjustment of them all, would it not? If you want the great piston of the engine to run with absolute freedom, give it absolutely perfect alignment and adjustment with the other parts of the engine, so that it is free, not because it is let alone or isolated, but because it has been associated most skillfully and carefully with the other parts of the great structure.

What is liberty? You say of the locomotive that it runs free. What do you mean? You mean that its parts are so assembled and adjusted that friction is reduced to a minimum, and that it has perfect adjustment. We say of a boat skimming the water with light foot, "How free she runs," when we mean, how perfectly she is adjusted to the force of the wind, how perfectly she obeys the great breath out of the heavens that fills her sails. Throw her head up into the wind and see how she will halt and stagger, how every sheet will shiver and her whole frame be shaken, how instantly she is "in irons," in the expressive phrase of the sea. She is free only when you have let her fall off again and have recovered once more her nice adjustment to the forces she must obey and cannot defy.

Human freedom consists in perfect adjustments of human interests and human activities and human energies.   [Woodrow Wilson, *The New Freedom*, 1915.]

Explanation of relationships

In exposition by explanation of relationships, you elucidate your subject by delineating clearly its place in the "scheme of things." For instance, you can explain quite effectively the "yield" signs on the highways by pinpointing their place on the scale between the sign that issues a command and the sign that merely guides. You can demonstrate, in brief, the relative function of the "yield" sign by showing how it differs from the sign requiring a full stop ("thru traffic stop"), the sign that merely warns ("bridge freezes before highway"), and the sign that guides ("Monterrey bear right"). In the course of your explanation, you naturally establish the relationship that the "yield" sign bears to the others.

Note how, in the following selection, the author explains his subject by comparing it to related subjects.

● Novocain or no, dental bills are likely to hurt all the way down to the innermost recesses of your wallet. The simple extraction or cleaning that a dozen years ago ran $5 or so now costs about twice that much. Extensive oral surgery for yourself or teeth straightening for your children can easily escalate to three or four figures. If the average family spends perhaps just $100 annually for dental care, it's only because so many families simply avoid checkups and let their teeth go.

For some fortunate Americans, about 16,000,000 in all, the financial sting is now being eased by some kind of dental insurance or prepayment plan. (That's about 14,000,000 more than were covered in 1965.) Roughly half are covered under commercial insurance policies, another fourth by dental service corporations organized by state dental societies, and the remainder under a variety of local setups, including group practices and clinics as well as nonprofit and self-insured plans.

Dental insurance isn't insurance in the usual sense of the word. When you buy coverage for accidents, fires or regular health hazards, for example, you're safeguarding yourself against problems that may or may not occur; the odds are long that the company will never have to ante up in any big way. But nearly everybody has difficulties, great or small, with his teeth or gums. With the young, the major culprit is decay. From middle age onward, the greatest problem is pyorrhea, a disease that inflames and loosens the gums, opening the way to bone deterioration. So dental insurance is more a method for preparing for a probable expense than protecting against an unlikely event.

If the decision to buy or not buy such insurance were left to individuals, those families with existing or expected problems would quite likely sign up while those with healthy teeth would not. That's one reason why virtually all dental insurance is written on a group rather than an individual basis. If entire groups are signed up, such as the employes at a plant, you get some participants with good teeth, some with bad, some with dentures. Spreading the risk in this manner is an important way of keeping costs down.

Another factor insurers rely on to pare expenses is dental neglect. Nobody really likes to go to the dentist, but if you pay good money for an individual plan, chances are you will use it. The motivation is not nearly so strong among those enrolled in a group, particularly one in which the employer foots all or most of the bill. Perhaps only 50% of those eligible will make use of available services. It has been estimated that if everyone who was qualified for dental services used them to the hilt, most dental insurance plans would go broke. ["Insurance that Pays the Dentist's Bills," *Changing Times*, September 1972.]

The five classifications discussed above are based on primary function; that is, a given example of expository writing falls within a specific class only because its main function so dictates. But in reality, most expository writing employs two or more of the techniques described.

This point can be illustrated by considering a long article in a health magazine on the subject of the cholesterol count in the human body. To accomplish his purpose, the author must explain the nature of cholesterol in body chemistry and the method of making a count (exposition by definition); he must discuss various foods in terms of the amount of cholesterol they supply to the human system (exposition by comparison); and he must discuss the place of cholesterol in human nutrition (exposition by explaining relationships). Throughout, of course, the author is also explaining by analyzing and by clarifying. Hence all five approaches are combined.

13.

Argument

Argument is basically an attempt to persuade or convince the reader to accept a particular viewpoint or conclusion. It presents the facts of a specific case in a manner that aims to lead the reader to accept the author's point of view. Ideally, argument places its entire emphasis on reason, even though an element of emotion exists in all but the most scientific of discussions.

Examples of argument are a magazine article by a conservationist pleading for preservation of forest areas, an editorial in a local newspaper supporting a referendum on an appropriation to build new schools, a health association pamphlet advocating certain practices leading to greater physical well-being for middle-aged citizens, and a student newspaper column asking for reconsideration of the college's "cut" system.

The term "argument" covers an extensive range of stylistic approaches. At one extreme is the argument of the lawyer who amasses an array of facts to be presented with appropriate oratory in the hope of winning his case; at the other is the lightly written essay extolling golf as an exercise for middle-aged people. At the one extreme is the richly embossed discourse by the polished writer who draws on great works of literature to support his statements; at the other is the simply phrased, direct approach of the physician-columnist warning his readers of the dangers of becoming overweight. Between these extremes are many types of writing that attempt to persuade or convince by sharply varied means.

In the passage below, one of America's most outspoken critics is arguing for a better understanding of our educational system.

● If the public, the teachers, and the professors all understood the educational system, we could develop a tradition in this country that would be far more effective in giving us the kind of education we need than laws, witch-hunts, or regulations that teachers must subscribe to oaths that, as Governor Warren of California has said, any traitor would take with a laugh. On the side of the teachers and professors, the professional tradition would mean that they taught responsibly. On the side of the public the tradition would mean that the public restrained itself in the exercise of its legal control.

Because I am concerned with the development of this tradition I deplore every futile, childish, and irrelevant activity in which the educational system engages. Educators do things that the public wants in order to get the support of the public. They do little to explain to the public why it should not want the things it does. I like intercollegiate football, but I recommended its abolition at Chicago, because the game in its industrial, big-time form has nothing to do with education and yet has the effect of diverting everybody's attention from the educational problems with which universities should be wrestling. So I deplore the multiplication of trivial courses, in cosmetology, fishing, and tapdancing, which swell the catalogues of great American universities and which have no purpose except to help the student while away four years without using his mind. Think of the most futile, childish, irrelevant subject you can—think of parlor games, think of self-beautification, think of anything you like—I will undertake to find it for you among the courses offered by American institutions of higher learning.   [Robert Maynard Hutchins, "Adjustment to the Environment," 1953.]

Collecting evidence for argument

Because evidence is the foundation upon which argument is built, you must exercise care in assembling the data and other material to be used in supporting your argument.

In most situations, more evidence exists than can be incorporated into an argument; therefore, you must learn how to make selections. If, for example, you were to argue for improved education in urban schools, you could easily find a storehouse of evidence to support your stand. Yet in the interest of brevity and effectiveness of presentation, you would have to choose whatever you deem most appropriate. For instance, there is clear proof that the higher the level of academic accomplishment, the better the care pupils tend to give their buildings. Therefore, improved education would lower the cost of building maintenance. This finding, however, cannot rank with more important reasons—for example, a democratic society owes every citizen the right to a good education. As a result, you would ignore the weak evidence in favor of the strong.

Equally important, you must select evidence in terms of the particular audience for which you are writing. For example, in arguing for educational reform before the parents of teenagers, you would stress the evidence that touches on teenagers. To childless people of late middle age, you would employ evidence of a more general nature.

A third consideration in selecting evidence is that it must be tested for factual soundness. You must check and double check on any doubtful facts; you must know something of the integrity and reliability of any source (book, magazine, etc.) from which you take data; and you must beware common misconceptions. Any error detected by your reader can cancel out the effectiveness of your entire argument.

A fourth point to bear in mind is that you must ascertain whether every piece of evidence is complete in itself and relevant to your argument. For instance, the fact that a young man is barely five feet tall has no bearing on his ambition to become an accountant; but it may have some bearing on his desire to be elected to high public office, and it definitely has considerable bearing on his intention of playing center on the college basketball team. Therefore, viewed as part of an argument, the young man's stature is an extraneous consideration in the first instance, may be a relevant consideration in the second, and is clearly a relevant consideration in the third.

Study the evidence the two well known authors below have collected to substantiate the stands they take. In the first selection, the writer supports his judgment on the quality of an important novel by citing evidence from the book itself. In the second selection, the writer relies on unchallengeable data to make his point.

Note also the use made in each selection of philosophical concepts as supports for the arguments presented.

- *The Grapes of Wrath* is a superb tract because it exposes something terrible and true with enormous vigor. It is a superb tract, moreover, by virtue of being thoroughly animated fiction, by virtue of living scenes and living characters (like Ma), not by virtue of discursive homilies and dead characters (like the socialistic preacher). One comes away moved, indignant, protesting, pitying. But one comes away dissatisfied, too, aware that *The Grapes of Wrath* is too unevenly weighted, too uneconomically proportioned, the work of a writer who is still self-indulgent, still undisciplined, still not altogether aware of the difference in value of various human emotions. The picturesqueness of the Joads, for example, is fine wherever it makes them live more abundantly, but false when simply laid on for effect. Steinbeck's sentimentalism is good in bringing him close to the lives of his people, but bad when it blurs his insight. Again, the chapters in which Steinbeck halts the story to editorialize about American life are sometimes useful, but oftener pretentious and flatulent.

  But one does not take leave of a book like this in a captious spirit. One salutes it as a fiery document of protest and compassion, as a story that had to be told, as a book that must be read. It is, I think, one of those books—there are not very many—which really do some good.   [Louis Kronenberger, "Hungry Caravan: A Review of *The Grapes of Wrath*," 1939.]

- An important fact about television—regardless of its sponsorship—is that you can have no interaction with it. A child sitting in front of a television set gets no experience in influencing behavior and being influenced in return. Having a puppy is in this sense far more important to a child than having a television set, although of course there is no reason he should not have both. The child who watches television for four hours daily between the ages of three and eighteen spends something like 22,000 hours in passive contemplation of the screen—hours stolen from the time needed to learn to relate to siblings, playmates, parents, grandparents, or strangers. Is there any connection between this fact and the sudden appearance in the past few years of an enormous number of young people from educated and middle-class families who find it difficult or impossible to relate to anybody—and therefore drop out?   [S. I. Hayakawa, "Who's Bringing Up Your Children?" 1968.]

Preparing the case in argument

There are five major procedures for presenting an argument in a logical fashion. They are (1) argument by presentation of pertinent evidence, (2) argument by analogy, (3) argument by inductive reasoning, (4) argument by deductive reasoning, and (5) argument by past experience.

Presentation of pertinent evidence employs a chain of facts or evidence to support a specific conclusion; that is, it is a process of amassing and presenting data to substantiate a main idea.

You employ this procedure, for example, when you argue that children should not be allowed to use skate boards on city streets because (1) the child can easily be injured by passing cars, (2) the child cannot control the skate board properly while watching for vehicular traffic, (3) the child can cause automobile accidents by forcing cars to swerve.

In preparing your case, you have three strong but distinctly separate arguments. These arguments you arrange in a one-two-three order—preceded by an introduction, followed by a conclusion, and held together by transitional elements.

The following selection illustrates the practice of arguing by presentation of pertinent evidence. The author contends that science must bear responsibility for the manner in which modern wars are fought. In the first paragraph, he introduces his viewpoint or main argument; in the succeeding three paragraphs, he presents the evidence to support his contention; and in the fifth paragraph, he summarizes and reiterates his stand.

● The sense of doom in us today is not a fear of science; it is a fear of war. And the causes of war were not created by science; they do not differ in kind from the known causes of the War of Jenkins' Ear or the Wars of the Roses, which were carried on with only the most modest scientific aids. No, science has not invented war; but it has turned it into a very different thing. The people who distrust it are not wrong. The man in the pub who says "It'll wipe out the world," the woman in the queue who says "It isn't natural"—they do not express themselves very well; but what they are trying to say does make sense. Science has enlarged the mechanism of war, and it has distorted it. It has done this in at least two ways.

First, science has obviously multiplied the power of the warmakers. The weapons of the moment can kill more people more secretly and more unpleasantly than those of the past. . . .

Secondly, science at the same time has given the nations quite new occasions for falling out. I do not mean such simple objectives as someone else's uranium mine, or a Pacific Island which happens to be knee-deep in organic fertilizer. . . .

I myself think there is a third dimension which science has added to modern war. It has created war nerves and the war of nerves. . . .

These are the indictments which scientists cannot escape. Of course, they are often badly phrased, so that scientists can side-step them with generalities about the common responsibility, and who voted the credits for atomic research anyway; which are perfectly just, but not at all relevant.   [Jacob Bronowski, *The Common Sense of Science*, 1956.]

Argument by analogy is generally used as a device within a main argument rather than as the principal approach of the total writing.

For example, if you argue for tighter automobile traffic laws, you may well use several analogies of widely different natures to prove your points. You may draw a parallel between reckless drivers and emotionally disturbed people; you may liken speeding cars to dangerous beasts on the loose; or you may compare the problems of heavily crowded highways to those of heavily crowded buildings.

On the other hand, in an argument for an enlarged school system to accommodate an expanding population, you may select a single analogy—such as that of preparing for a hurricane that is indisputably on its way—and discuss your subject in terms of this comparison.

Below are two instances of argument by analogy. In the first, Frank Norris draws analogies between the novelist and the Wall Street businessman and between the novelist and the newspaper reporter. In the second passage, the writer makes his point by employing an analogy that compares the use of drugs with the use of cigarettes.

● And truth in fiction is just as real and just as important as truth anywhere else—as in Wall Street, for instance. A man who does not tell the truth there, and who puts the *un*truth upon paper over his signature will be very promptly jailed. In the case of the Wall Street man the sum of money in question may be trivial, a hundred dollars, fifty dollars. But the untruthful novelist who starts in motion something like half a million dollars invokes not fear nor yet reproach. If truth in the matter of the producing of novels is not an elusive, intangible abstraction, what then is it? Let us get at the hard nub of the business, something we can hold in the hand. It is the thing that is one's own, the discovery of a subject suitable for fictitious narration that has never yet been treated, and the conscientious study of that subject and the fair presentation of results. Not a difficult matter it would appear, not an abstraction, not a philosophical kink. Newspaper reporters, who are not metaphysicians, unnamed, unrewarded, despised even and hooted and hounded, are doing this every day. They do it on a meagre salary, and they call the affair a "scoop." Is the standard of the novelist—he who is entrusted with the good name of his nation's literature—lower than that of a reporter?   ["The Responsibilities of the Novelist," 1903.]

● There is still a powerful premise circulating among educators that individuals, especially children, can be *frightened* away from drugs with "proper information about dangers." In all frankness, this hope is a utopian fantasy. Before anyone gets optimistic about the value of "dynamic, hard-hitting facts" in a drug abuse curriculum, he should give careful thought to the remarkable staying power of cigarettes in the mature adult population, despite the demonstrated dangers.

In vew of this fact, does it seem reasonable to expect a "scare" campaign to be decisive? The young are more non-rational, risk-oriented, and unbelieving... [Allan Y. Cohen, "Alternatives to Drug Use," PTA, September 1972.]

Arguing by inductive reasoning means arguing from the particular to the general. To illustrate: if you argue that because the residents of a particular city are concerned about world affairs (the particular), most city-dwellers feel the same concern (the general), you are arguing inductively.

When arguing inductively, you must be sure your evidence meets the criterion of representativeness. Representativeness is measured by answering such questions as how extensive a group, how wide an area, and how great a situation does this evidence represent? You can find, for example, an occasional American child who does not like ice cream, but you can scarcely prove that such a child is representative of a large number of children. Similarly, you can sometimes find a low-price car that has given its owner over 100,000 miles of service without major repair bills. However, such a car represents a very small percentage of its class.

In the following selection, the writer argues from the particular (the fact that Russia is restricting the emigration of college-educated Jews) to the general (the fact that Russia may eventually place similar restrictions on the emigration of all college-educated people) in the hope of stressing the inherent dangers in the total situation.

● No doubt the so-called exit tax being imposed by Russia on college educated Jews who want to emigrate to Israel is another form of ransom, as claimed by Israeli Prime Minister Golda Meir. But other factors may be involved, too.

Jews, because of their heritage, are perceptive and sensitive when it comes to analyzing oppressors. Allowing highly educated Jews to leave Russia opens the way for a convincing exposure of the Russian system.

In addition, the emigration of the Russian Jews to Israel is a form of aid to a long standing Mideast enemy at a time when the Arab world, particularly Egypt, is showing signs of loosening ties with the Russians.

There is also the problem, common to many countries, of the "brain drain."

Is Russia simply, or as part of a more complex plan, trying to keep its best educated people through the clumsy device of an exit tax rather than by improving living conditions?

As far as we know, the tax is being imposed only on emigrating Jews. But that could be because the Jews are in the unique situation of having a new homeland to go to. But conceivably, the tax could be applied to other Russians, now or in the future, as a device for making emigration less attractive and thus maintaining a Soviet intellectual base. [" 'Brain Drain' Plug?" *The Milwaukee Sentinel*, August 22, 1972.]

Argument by deductive reasoning means argument from the general to the particular. It is easy to illustrate this widely employed type of argument. When you argue that all men must learn as best they can to combat the vicissitudes of life, you are arguing deductively. You are saying that because all human history demonstrates that life is one long series of trials (the general), every man must learn how to battle these trials if he is to live purposefully and happily (the particular).

An especially helpful device in arguing deductively is the *syllogism*, which is composed of three main parts: major premise, minor premise, and conclusion. These parts are employed as follows:

Major premise: All normal men desire a measure of acclaim.

Minor premise: Jim is a normal man.

Conclusion: Jim desires a measure of acclaim.

The two paragraphs below have been extracted from a student

theme. Note how the writer employs two syllogisms to make his point.

- In the past several weeks, I have become very disillusioned about this college. I have been asking myself a series of questions which have returned nothing but distressing answers. Isn't the primary function of a college that of providing a first-class education? Answer, yes. Is this college providing a first-class education? Answer, no. Then, is something seriously wrong? Answer, definitely yes.

  Next, I ask myself if students, the buyers, should have the right to complain about faulty merchandise, their education, to the sellers, the administration. The answer is clearly yes. That brings up the question, do the students on this campus have the opportunity to register their complaints, and the answer is once again, no. All this leads to the inescapable conclusion that the students on this campus are being denied a basic right.

The passage below is a good example of deductive reasoning. In this writing, the author presents a general statement in his first two sentences. Then he proceeds to argue his point by citing specific instances as substantiation. Hence he has gone from a general to a specific.

- Patriotism may not always be the last refuge of a scoundrel, but it is too often a convenient disguise for a one-hundred-per-center who wants somebody else to go back home. Nor are radicals without guile. If the La Follette committee has turned the spotlight on reactionaries whose favorite reading matter is the Constitution whenever they import plug-uglies to break a strike, I have noted a wonderful interest in the Bill of Rights among communists in danger of arrest and deportation. The devil can cite Scripture for his purpose. There is scarcely a pressure group in the country that cannot cite Jefferson or Lincoln, Washington or Wilson, in support of a quiet little programme of its own.   [Howard Mumford Jones, "Patriotism—But How?" *The Atlantic*, 1938.]

Argument by past experience uses the past to build a case for or against a present or future action or event. When, for instance, you argue that the nation can expect a period of recession because of the cyclic nature of the economy, you are arguing on the basis of past experience. When you argue that older people are generally more resistant to social and similar changes, you base your judgment on past experience.

The following passage illustrates argument by past experience. In this selection, the writer is arguing that the critics of advertising are really attacking the competitive process. To accomplish his purpose, he cites practices, customs, and philosophical viewpoints that have characterized the American public as well as truths and laws commonly accepted by economists.

● The critics of advertising are really attacking the competitive process. Competition involves considerable duplication and "waste." The illustrations range from the several gasoline stations at an important intersection to the multiplication of research facilities, the excess industrial capacity which develops during periods of expansion, and the accumulations of excessive inventories.

We cannot judge the efficiency of our competitive society— including the various instrumentalities, such as advertising—by looking at the negative aspects alone. It is true that competition involves waste. But it also yields a flood of new products, improved quality, better service, and pressures on prices. In the United States, it has facilitated enormous economic growth with the accompanying high standards of living. The advantages of competition have been so overwhelmingly greater than the wastes that we have established as one of our prime national goals the continuance of a competitive economy.   [Jules Backman, *Advertising and Competition*, 1967.]

Regardless of the procedures or techniques employed, the writer of argument must constantly observe this guideline: because argument always reflects in some way, however small, elements of the writer's personality, the writer must guard zealously against any over-aggressiveness, superciliousness, or other offensive attribute. In other words, he must try to strike the reader as the kind of person one enjoys associating with on a day-to-day basis.

Note how the author of the following passage has prevented himself from becoming obtrusive.

● Dr. James Grigson was the state's only witness. As usual, he was enough. At issue was whether to execute Ernest Smith, a 26-year-old man who had been convicted of murder for robbing a convenience store in Dallas and standing by while his partner shot and killed the clerk. Under Texas law, the jury had to decide at the sentencing hearing whether there was "a probability that the defendant would commit criminal acts of violence that would constitute a continuing threat to society." It seemed a difficult question—Smith, after all, had no previous criminal record of violence. His only other arrest had been for marijuana possession. But Grigson had a clear-cut answer.

"Certainly Mr. Smith is going to go ahead and commit other similar or same criminal acts if given the opportunity to do so," Grigson testified. His training as a psychiatrist, he explained, enabled him to conclude from a 90-minute interview with Smith that the defendant was an incorrigible "sociopath," a man who felt no remorse for his crime. The jury voted for the death sentence, just as more than 70 other Texas juries have done in other capital cases at which Grigson offered similar testimony. Only three times had a jury heard Grigson testify and not recommended capital punishment. Defense attorneys in Texas call him "Dr. Death."

Smith's lawyers protested the verdict, and so did the American Psychiatric Association. Psychiatrists' long-term predictions about criminal behavior should be barred from court, the association argued in a legal brief, because such testimony "gives the appearance of being based on expert medical judgment, when in fact no such expertise exists." While it may have seemed surprising for a professional group to be debunking the abilities of its own members, the association's stance was hardly radical. Virtually every research study in the past decade has shown that when it comes to making long-term predictions about behavior, psychiatrists are wrong more often than they are right. Yet the courts continue to seek opinions in tens of thousands of cases a year, creating what is probably the most serious problem in forensic psychiatry today.   [John Tierney, "Doctor, Is This Man Dangerous?" *Science 82*, June 1982.]

Part Three

The writing process

14.

Formulating your thoughts

The writing process encompasses the entire procedure of preparing a paper or report. Generally speaking, the process involves four steps: (1) reflection, (2) organizing, (3) composing the rough draft, and (4) revising for the final copy.

Reflection is the broad, general thinking the writer does after selecting a topic and doing all the necessary research. For some writing, the process may be quite brief. For the formal essay and similar writing, the process is likely to be much more detailed.

If your writing demands extensive reflection, you should observe certain cautions.

Above all, you should remember that reflective thought cannot be hurried. It must be allowed to move at its own slow, natural pace. If you are to write, for example, about your definition of success, you must deliberate at length; you cannot formulate your thoughts capably if you hurry. Hence you should try to reflect on your topic during every free moment—when you are walking along the street, when you are resting, whenever you have a chance to think without sudden interruption. In this way, you will find the subject coming into focus at odd times. Perhaps as you pause in the midst of other work, a significant point will crop up; perhaps as you are having dinner, an important idea will flash through your mind. Of one fact you can be certain: if you postpone reflection until the last moment, you will still be thinking of central ideas long after the paper is out of your hands.

While you reflect you must be open to associations that can lead you to previously unthought of aspects of the topic. To illustrate: you are assigned the topic cited above—your definition of success. You realize that the concept is fundamentally subjective, and ideas on the subject are certain to vary; therefore, definitions will vary. By deduction, you realize that your own definition has changed many times and that it probably will continue to change as you grow older. You have formulated another major point. From there, your pattern of association leads you to the fact that a person's later life is strongly influenced by his early definitions of success (a college student's choice of curriculum, for example, results in large part from his views of success). Now you have still another essential thought. Pressing further, you discern the all-encompassing impact of each person's definition on his every activity, now and later. Hence you see that each person's concept of success is the keystone of his life. Throughout the period of reflection, each point has led through association to a more extensive, more thorough consideration of the topic.

In attempting to press into all corners of a topic, you should ask yourself leading questions. Have I covered every angle? Are some of my thoughts trivial? Are some apparently extraneous points actually relevant? And above all, you should try to see every fact in perspective.

One of the best ways to strengthen your own case is to examine each point and anticipate and seek answers to any opposing arguments. In discussing success, for example, anticipate the frequent statement that any definition is certain to be wholly subjective. You should then be prepared to demonstrate that despite the presence of a strong subjective note, a person's definition of success is more than mere personal opinion; it is based in part on objective elements. Among these objective elements is the demonstrable fact that normal people must feel they are contributing to the welfare of society in order to feel they are successful. Therefore, an element of altruism must be present in any normal person's definition of success. Thus, you strengthen your own case by answering probable objections to it.

When reflecting on your topic, you should make notes, even

though they may seem sketchy and unorganized. The reason is that most people tend to overestimate the powers of their memories; they assume that they can remember far more facts than they do. Therefore, a writer who makes no notes during reflection may obtain important points, only to lose them through a normal process of forgetting.

While recording your thoughts, watch carefully for particularly expressive phrases or precise words that can be used to strengthen the final draft. Quite often, during these periods of reflection, a telling word or phrase may occur to you only to be forgotten later. If you record this material, you have it when you need it.

Finally, do not assume that reflection and writing are always pleasant undertakings. Rather, as so many famous writers have said, they are frequently difficult and enervating experiences. They are often a series of trials, pressures, and problems that can be almost overwhelming at times. To understand this situation, you should be aware of the meaning of the phrase, the "paradox of the creative act." Because this phrase is not so widely known as it deserves, some explanation is in order. On the one hand, artists—painters, sculptors, writers, or other artists—declare that they love their art, that they could not live without the opportunity to create. On the other hand, as they engage in the actual production, they often suffer acute discomfort.

As they paint, sculpt, or write, artists frequently experience exhausting turmoil and stress. Nonetheless, they press on to complete their creation. Then, surveying the finished product, they may feel a surge of satisfaction, experience a sensation often called the "joy of accomplishment." All the pain of planning and executing the project, all the discomfort, all the pressure become submerged in a glow of satisfaction derived from beholding the creation itself.

As a writer, you should be aware of this paradox because as you probe endlessly for your thoughts, as you search for just the right word, or as you struggle to improve a knotty sentence, you may well wonder how anyone could ever enjoy writing. Yet when you produce a soundly prepared work, you, like writers great and insignificant, will know the paradox of the creative act.

15.

Planning your paper

The four principal types of writing—narration, description, exposition, and argument—entail clearly different kinds of planning.

Narration

In narration, unlike the other three forms, the broad structure evolves naturally from the material itself. Organizing material is, therefore, largely a matter of detecting and following the narrative thread. This statement means that because narration is the recounting of an incident or a story, the events fall into a natural chronological sequence. You determine the place of each incident in the story, thereby obtaining your structure.*

This point can be illustrated with a rather unusual incident. A circus elephant, tethered to a stake, has broken away shortly after midnight and somehow has made its way undetected to the center of the city, where it suddenly appears at the height of morning traffic. Police officers, striving earnestly but unprofessionally to handle the situation, inadvertently arouse the elephant and cause

---

*The term "narration," as discussed in this section, refers to narrative writing of a literary nature. The term does not cover factual report writing cast in a narrative approach (for example, the account of a test flight of a new airplane).

157

him to trot and trumpet through the crowded streets for almost an hour before circus personnel, speeded to the scene in a police emergency vehicle, bring the elephant under control and lead him away.

The main incidents in this narrative are (1) a circus elephant suddenly appears at the height of morning traffic at a busy intersection; (2) police attempt to control the elephant but succeed only in scaring him into trotting and trumpeting through the streets; (3) circus personnel speed to the scene in a police emergency vehicle; and (4) the circus personnel bring the elephant under control and lead him away.

You, the writer, must isolate these points as the main supports of the narrative structure and then enlarge upon each point properly by introducing appropriate detail—for example, the elephant was able to uproot the stake because the surrounding earth was soft, the actual mistakes made by the police in arousing the elephant, terrified reactions of some motorists and pedestrians.

In the opinion of most professional short story writers, knowing how to isolate and handle all the pertinent detail within a narrative situation is a matter of "feeling" the story. These authors contend that to write a successful story, a writer must be able to sense instinctively the total structure of the story, the relationship of events to each other, and the elements of cohesiveness (supporting detail, etc.) that hold the story together. Therefore, before you can relate a story you must be able to feel it.

Note how successfully the writers have sensed the narrative elements in the passages below. Note, also, how they have discerned the relationship that each event and thought bears to the others—as well as how everything is joined into one cohesive unit.

● We were a week working up as far as Yarmouth Roads, and then we got into a gale—the famous October gale of twenty-two years ago. It was wind, lightning, sleet, snow and a terrific sea. We were flying light, and you may imagine how bad it was when I tell you we had smashed bulwarks and a flooded deck. On the second night she shifted her ballast into the ice bow, and by that time we had been blown off somewhere on the Dogger Bank. There was nothing for it but go below with shovels and try to right her, and there we were in that vast hold, gloomy like a cavern, the tallow dips stuck and flickering on the beams, the gale howling above, the ship tossing about like mad on her side; there we all were, Jermyn, the captain, every one, hardly able to keep our feet, engaged on that gravedigger's work, and trying to toss shovelfuls of wet sand up to windward. At every tumble of the ship you could see vaguely in the dim light men falling down with a great flourish of shovels. One of the ship's boys (we had two), impressed by the weirdness of the scene, wept as if his heart would break. We could hear him blubbering somewhere in the shadows.   [Joseph Conrad, *Youth*, 1902.]

• The barrier was down at the railway crossing. An express was coming from the station. Marya Vasilyevna stood at the crossing waiting for the train to pass, and shivering all over with cold. Vyazovye was in sight now, and the school with the green roof, and the church with its blazing crosses that reflected the setting sun; and the station windows were aflame, too, and a pink smoke rose from the engine. And it seemed to her that everything was shivering with cold.

Here was the train; the windows, like the crosses on the church, reflected the blazing light; it hurt her eyes to look at them. On the platform of one of the first-class carriages a lady was standing, and Marya Vasilyevna glanced at her as she flashed by. Her mother! What a resemblance! Her mother had had just such luxuriant hair, just such a forehead and that way of holding her head. And with amazing distinctness, for the first time in those thirteen years, she imagined vividly her mother, her father, her brother, their apartment in Moscow, the aquarium with the little fishes, everything down to the smallest detail; she suddenly heard the piano playing, her father's voice; she felt as then, young, good-looking, well-dressed, in a bright warm room among her own people. A feeling of joy and happiness suddenly overwhelmed her, she pressed her hands to her temples in ecstasy, and called softly, imploringly:

"Mama!"

And she began to cry, she did not know why. Just at that moment Hanov drove up with his team of four horses, and seeing him she imagined such happiness as had never been, and smiled and nodded to him as an equal and an intimate, and it seemed to her that the sky, the windows, the trees, were glowing with her happiness, her triumph. No, her father and mother had never died, she had never been a schoolmistress, that had been a long, strange, oppressive dream, and now she had awakened.

"Vasilyevna, get in!"

And suddenly it all vanished. The barrier was slowly rising. Marya Vasilyevna, shivering and numb with cold, got into the cart. The carriage with the four horses crossed the railway track. Semyon followed. The guard at the crossing took off his cap.   [Anton Chekhov, "In the Cart," 1902.]

Narrative writing—like exposition, description, and argument—is divided into three parts: introduction, body, and conclusion.

The *introduction* (1) sets the stage for the events that follow, (2) generates interest, and (3) creates atmosphere.

In very short narratives, the introduction may be implied rather than stated. Note how the opening sentence in the following passage presents pertinent detail while it introduces by implication.

● Not long ago an airline president had planned a special flight for leading publishers and others. It was an ultra-important occasion. To everyone's relief, arrangements clicked perfectly on the day of departure. Passengers and baggage were whisked through customs with a minimum of red tape. Fluttering staff members and public officials lent an aura of excitement to the scene. Guests were briefed and seated. The airline president was beaming his satisfaction. Crew members were at stations. The big props turned over and speeded up. All was set.

Then suddenly the props throttled back and stopped. The ramp was pushed to the door again. The door opened and all looked back. A grim face poked into the cabin and a blunt voice announced, "This airplane won't take off today."

It was the voice of the Chief Mechanic. He had found an oil leak.

Who runs an airline? Did the president fume at the Chief Mechanic? Not he. "Thank you, Chief," he said, and de-planed his guests for a luncheon downtown and a departure later in the day in another aircraft. So who runs an airline? Here again it is safety alone that delegates authority ...   [Howard G. Kurtz, Jr., "Toward Tomorrow," 1955.]

In longer narratives, the introduction is, of course, more extensive and more formally conceived. Below are four introductions from well known short stories.

- As Mr. John Oakhurst, gambler, stepped into the main street of Poker Flat on the morning of the 23d of November, 1850, he was conscious of a change in its moral atmosphere since the preceding night. Two or three men, conversing earnestly together, ceased as he approached, and exchanged significant glances. There was a Sabbath lull in the air, which, in a settlement unused to Sabbath influences, looked ominous. [Bret Harte, "The Outcasts of Poker Flat," 1869.]

- In the year 1799, Captain Amasa Delano, of Duxbury, in Massachusetts, commanding a large sealer and general trader, lay at anchor with a valuable cargo, in the harbor of St. Maria—a small, deserted, uninhabited island toward the southern extremity of the long coast of Chile. There he had touched for water.   [Herman Melville, "Benito Cereno," 1855.]

- Conscious as I am of a deep aversion to stories of a painful nature, I have often asked myself whether, in the events here set forth, the element of pain is stronger than that of joy. An affirmative answer to this question would have stood as a veto upon the publication of my story, for it is my opinion that the literature of horrors needs no extension.   [Henry James, "My Friend Bingham," 1867.]

- Lily, the caretaker's daughter, was literally run off her feet. Hardly had she brought one gentleman into the pantry behind the office on the ground floor and helped him off with his overcoat than the wheezy hall-door bell clanged again and she had to scamper along the bare hallway to let in another guest. It was well for her she had not to attend to the ladies also.   [James Joyce, "The Dead," 1916.]

In handling the second part of narrative writing, the *body*, the most serious problem is selection of detail. Because using all the facts available is usually both unnecessary and harmful, the writer must learn to make proper selections; he must know the facts to retain, those to modify, and those to eliminate.

In making his selections, he must respect two considerations: (1) indispensability in recounting the story fully and (2) strength in contributing to atmosphere.

The importance of selecting narrative detail is easy to appreciate. Imagine an appealing story without one or more of its essential facts. Or, conversely, think of a long-winded account that could be improved by pruning excess facts and detail.

Proper handling of detail can be illustrated by the selection below. Note how the italicized facts can be omitted without loss to the narrative element.

- Yesterday when I returned to my dormitory, I found a visitor waiting for me in the lobby. He was a tall, stout man, about fifty, who informed me that he had a very important matter to discuss with me. *He was wearing a gray suit with a white shirt and blue tie*, and his manner was both impressive and somewhat terrifying.

  We moved over to the corner of the reception room where he opened a briefcase and began to speak in soft, confidential tones. He seemed to know all about me as he gave details of my age, place of residence, and family background. All the while, he scanned the room to make certain that no one was within earshot.

  Becoming somewhat apprehensive, I demanded to know who he was and what he wanted. He merely turned my questions aside with a gesture of postponement. After several minutes, however, the truth emerged. He was an insurance salesman who was there to sell me a policy—the first payment for which was to be due one month after graduation.

  I showed him the door—fast.

It is difficult to decide what *detail should be included for the sake of atmosphere*. For example, ask a few simple questions regarding the writing above. Instead of discarding the description of the insurance salesman's clothing, should the writer not only have retained it but added further detail? Would such detail have created a deeper atmosphere for the story? Might not, for example, a carefully wrought description of the man's fingernails, his style of haircut, and his choice of jewelry create a more conducive atmosphere in which to recount the story? Might not the impact of the story be greater with such detail added for background? Certainly there is often a correlation between attire and personality. Therefore, why not include this detail, and supply additional detail as well?

The amount of detail used to create atmosphere is one of the noteworthy differences between typical nineteenth and twentieth century American short stories. Writers like Washington Irving, Nathaniel Hawthorne, and Herman Melville employed extensive detail to embellish the atmosphere of their stories. Most present-day short story writers, however, seem to concentrate on detail primarily as a means of weaving a narrative thread.

In deciding whether to use detail to create atmosphere, you must note a special caution: in some narrative writing, detail to create atmosphere is to be either minimized or entirely avoided. In narrative accounts of a factual nature the emphasis must naturally be on hard, unchallengeable fact. There is little or no place for the inclusion of detail to create atmosphere.

An illustration of this caution is evident in the passage presented below. In this selection, taken from a scholarly work, the author is recounting a situation rich in fictional possibilities. Because he is writing as a researcher, however, he must confine himself to firm, scientific data, purposely controlling any attempt to become dramatic, subjective, or otherwise nonscientific.

- The Family Founder was Meyer Guggenheim, who came to Philadelphia from his native Switzerland in 1847. He began by peddling shoe polish on the streets of the city, then branching out into the lace business, and finally laying the cornerstone of his fortune in mining and smelting. As no dynasty is based on money alone, it was fortunate that his wife bore him eleven children, including eight sons. This second generation, well disciplined by their father's weekly councils on Friday nights to outline family affairs and instill tradition, carried on the dynasty by enlarging the family businesses to include tin mines in Bolivia, gold mines in Alaska, diamond fields in Africa, copper mines and nitrate fields in Chile, and rubber plantations in the Congo. They also married into prominent families within their class and faith, and produced twenty-four children. There was only one divorce, which was forced on the youngest son because he had married someone the family considered unsuitable. [E. Digby Baltzell, *The Protestant Establishment*, 1964.]

The *conclusion* of the narrative writing may be either stated or implied. The writer states his conclusion when he feels that he must develop the high point of the story in order to give it a maximum impact. He implies it when he feels (1) it is so self-evident that to spell it out would affront the intelligence of his reader or (2) he can obtain a stronger impact by allowing the reader to see it for himself.

Below are three narrative writings. In the first, the conclusion is clearly stated; in the second and third, it is implied.

● In 1967, a twenty-three-year-old girl from Chickasaw County, Mississippi, went into a Hollywood recording studio and cut "demos" of two of her songs. After the demonstration cuts were transferred from magnetic tape to disk, she took the "dub" to Capitol Records. Although she had been singing and dancing in Los Angeles and Las Vegas clubs, Bobbie Lee Gentry was trying to sell her songs, not her singing. Capitol executives were so impressed by both, not to mention her good looks, that they signed her and released her "Ode to Billie Joe" backed with "Mississippi Delta" as her first disk. Within weeks, the tragic-blues tale of "Billie Joe" had outdistanced competitive records by The Monkees, The Supremes and others to become #1 on the record charts of all music tradepapers—*Billboard*, *Cash Box* and *Record World*. Overnight Miss Gentry became a new singing sensation whose voice was heard all over the radio dial, whose face was seen on major TV shows, and whose swift rise was celebrated in newspaper and magazine accounts. [Arnold Shaw, *The Rock Revolution*, New York, 1969.]

- Ludwig van Beethoven's 200th birthday has been celebrated this year with due reverence in much of the musical world. But the city of San Antonio is giving the anniversary song a definite Texas beat. The San Antonio Symphony, trying to raise $75,000 for its endowment fund, has found Ludwig a profitable gimmick. Recently, guests arriving for a fund-raising coffee were startled to be greeted by a smiling Beethoven who said, "Velcome to *mein* birthday." Actually, it was an actor named Stewart Drake, suited up in Viennese knickers and wig. The delighted guests sang "Happy birthday, dear Ludwig." Then there is the "Bucks for Beethoven" campaign, in which music lovers purchase specially printed funny money that shows the master flashing the V sign. This week the coda. The symphony fund raisers will have Drake-Beethoven auction off several bottles of liquor. The folks will be bidding for—what else?— "Beethoven's Fifth."   [*Time*, December 21, 1970.]

- Midway through the sixth game of the 1964 Stanley Cup finals against Detroit, Bobby Baun, then of the Toronto Maple Leafs, was hit on the leg by the puck and carried from the rink on a stretcher. In the training room he received an injection of Novocain. His leg was taped, he returned to play, and he scored the winning goal in overtime. The next day it was determined Baun had a cracked right fibula. Nonetheless, he was shot with painkiller and willingly, probably eagerly, took his regular turn on the ice the following day.

  Numbing a broken leg and sending the patient out to play hockey is not a treatment any physician would follow with a nonathlete. It may not cause complications, but the procedure has no known therapeutic value. It is not conceived as a method of speeding up or improving the knitting of bone. The only motive was to enable a man to play a game he could not otherwise have played.   [Bil Gilbert, "Athletes in a Turned-On World," *Sports Illustrated*, June 23, 1969.]

Description

There can be no such entity as pure description or pure exposition or pure argument. Each form invariably reflects elements of the other forms. The definition of each form, therefore, can be constructed only in terms of primary function: that is, description has, as its primary function, the aim of describing; exposition has, as its primary function, the aim of explaining; and argument has, as its primary function, the aim of persuading.* Consequently, in each instance, a label is assigned in terms of primary function.

The difficulties inherent in definitions become clear by reading a passage like that presented below. In it a well-known historian is refuting a popular misconception regarding French-American relations during the Revolutionary period. Although his primary aim is to explain, he obviously invokes elements of both description and argument. Furthermore, there is even an element of narration in this passage.

● A recent Broadway musical extravaganza reflects the romantic notions many Americans still entertain about the diplomacy of the American Revolution. According to this popular conception, America was so fortunate as to have a shrewd and benevolent sage in France to safeguard and promote her interests, a master diplomat whose democratic garb, severe Quaker black and beaver hat, made him stand out strikingly among the peacocks at Versailles, a man who could exploit flirtation to the advantage of patriotism, who could confound the most devious statesman in direct confrontation, and was able almost singlehandedly to persuade La Belle France to come to the rescue of American liberty for purposes largely altruistic. [Richard B. Morris, *The American Revolution*, 1967.]

As you plan a descriptive passage, you must separate the necessary or pertinent detail from the unnecessary detail, and you must decide upon an arrangement for the details. Think of yourself as a writer charged with the task of describing a local library. First you look at the building and determine that it is three stories high, approximately 100 feet long and 40 feet deep, of Gothic architecture, and of attractive appearance. These, of course, are the main

---

*You should also note that narration, for example, frequently contains strong elements of description, exposition, and argument.

features of the building and consequently become the main facts in your writing. In addition, you must settle on the lesser facts to be included.

Next, you decide upon a framework for describing these details. You know you cannot jump from one detail to another; rather, you must employ a logical and interesting framework so that your reader can follow the total writing knowledgeably and comfortably.

All frameworks or structures for descriptive writing follow four major organizing principles: (1) comparative importance order, (2) chronological order, (3) appearance order, and (4) space order. Each framework has advantages and disadvantages. As a result, the writer must choose in terms of the suitability of the particular order for his material.

Comparative importance order is that in which the writer describes the most important aspect first and then moves on to the lesser points, but, in some special cases, he may begin with the least important aspects and work up to those of greater significance.

When describing a courtroom, for example, the writer would naturally focus attention first on the judge's bench. Then on the defense and prosecution tables, the jury box, and the spectators' seats. Although a second person can dispute the relative importance of one place over another (for example, the defense table versus the prosecution table), the order represents the writer's conclusions regarding the relative importance of the areas involved.

In making an outline for this order, the writer begins with an introduction, followed by the details arranged in order of importance. A statement of summation or a conclusion closes the writing.

Below is a selection from the well-known Sir Roger de Coverly papers. It is considered to be one of the most adroit uses of the comparative importance order in all essay writing.

- The first of our society is a gentleman of Worcestershire, of ancient descent, a baronet, his name Sir Roger de Coverly. His great-grandfather was inventor of that famous country-dance which is called after him. All who know that shire are very well acquainted with the parts and merits of Sir Roger. He is a gentleman that is very singular in his behaviour, but his singularities proceed from his good sense, and are contradictions to the manners of the world, only as he thinks the world is in the wrong. However, this humour creates him no enemies, for he does nothing with sourness or obstinacy; and his being unconfined to modes and forms, makes him but the readier and more capable to please and oblige all who know him. When he is in town he lives in Soho Square: it is said, he keeps himself a bachelor by reason he was crossed in love by a perverse beautiful widow of the next county to him. Before this disappointment, Sir Roger was what you call a fine gentleman, had often supped with Lord Rochester and Sir George Etherege, fought a duel upon his first coming to town, and kicked Bully Dawson in a public coffee-house for calling him youngster. But being ill used by the above-mentioned widow, he was very serious for a year and a half; and though his temper being naturally jovial, he at last got over it, he grew careless of himself and never dressed afterwards; he continues to wear a coat and doublet of the same cut that were in fashion at the time of his repulse, which, in his merry humours, he tells us, has been in and out twelve times since he first wore it. He is now in his fifty-sixth year, cheerful, gay, and hearty, keeps a good house in both town and country; a great lover of mankind; but there is such a mirthful cast in his behaviour, that he is rather beloved than esteemed. His tenants grow rich, his servants look satisfied, all the young women profess love to him, and the young men are glad of his company; when he comes into a house he calls the servants by their names, and talks all the way up stairs to a visit. I must not omit that Sir Roger is a justice of the quorum; that he fills the chair at a quarter session with great abilities, and three months ago, gained universal applause by explaining a passage in the Game-Act.

The gentleman next in esteem and authority among us, is another bachelor, who is a member of the Inner Temple; a man of great probity, wit and understanding. . . .

The person of next consideration is Sir Andrew Freeport, a merchant of great eminence in the city of London: a person of indefatigable industry, strong reason, and great experience. . . .

Next to Sir Andrew in the club-room sits Captain Sentry, a gentleman of great courage, good understanding, but invincible modesty. . . .

But that our society may not appear a set of humourists unacquainted with the gallantries and pleasures of the age, we have among us the gallant Will. Honeycomb, a gentleman who, according to his years, should be in the decline of his life, but having ever been very careful of his person, and always had a very easy fortune, time has made but very little impression, either by wrinkles on his forehead, or traces in his brain. . . . [Richard Steele, "Of the Club," 1712.]

Like other arrangements, comparative importance order is frequently used in combination with other approaches. The paragraph below, for instance, is basically exposition because its primary purpose is to explain the concept of open education. In composing the passage, however, the author has relied heavily on a comparative importance order to describe classroom activity. His purpose is to explain the concept by describing, in order of importance as he sees the matter, the activities of the children in the classroom.

● Open education is based on the concept of childhood as something to be cherished—that it is not mere preparation for later schooling or life, but a vital part of life itself to be lived richly each day; that learning is more effective if it grows out of the interests of the learner in a free, supportive, non-threatening environment. Open education is based on the recognition that children are different, learn in different ways, at different times, and from each other. There is little uniformity in an open education classroom. Children move about freely, talk with each other, make choices, work alone or in small groups, and peruse materials relevant to them. There is no sign of mere busy work, meaningless drill, nor conformist activities. Materials in the open classroom include a rich range of textbooks, library books and reference books of varying difficulty, a multitude of audio-visual materials for children to use, quantities of materials for manipulation and experimentation, and supplies for music, art, and creative pursuits. The open classroom is rich in living plants and animals. There are provocative written and spoken questions posed by the teacher to stimulate children to think, test, describe, write, read, and figure. It is a happy learning environment for children.   [Ewald B. Nyquist, "Open Education," *The Science Teacher*, September 1971.]

Chronological order is the presentation of events or perceptions in the framework of time; that is, you arrange your details in terms of successive steps. Naturally, chronological order can be used only where a time pattern exists. For example, chronological order could not be used to describe the contents of a showcase; but it could be used effectively to describe the unveiling of a monument.

The passage below describes the arrival of a funeral train.

● Just then a distant whistle sounded, and there was a shuffling of feet on the platform. A number of lanky boys of all ages appeared as suddenly and slimily as eels wakened by the crack of thunder; some came from the waiting-room, where they had been warming themselves by the red stove, or half asleep on the slat benches; others uncoiled themselves from baggage trucks or slid out of express wagons. Two clambered down from the driver's seat of a hearse that stood backed up against the siding. They straightened their stooping shoulders and lifted their heads, and a flash of momentary animation kindled their dull eyes at that cold, vibrant scream, the world-wide call for men. It stirred them like the note of a trumpet; just as it had often stirred the man who was coming home tonight, in his boyhood. [Willa Cather, "The Sculptor's Funeral," 1931.]

Below is a passage from a college botany textbook that describes the increase in hybrid corn in the United States.

● Between 1909 and 1925, experimentation with hybrid corn was accelerated. Federal and state experiment stations joined in the research, and dozens of men gave the problem their full attention; others talked to farmers and wrote articles advocating the use of hybrid corn. Yet in 1933 the U.S. Department of Agriculture reported that only 0.1 percent of the corn planted in the United States was hybrid. In that year the average yield per acre was 22.6 bushels. Ten years later 51 percent of the corn planted was hybrid. By then the average yield had increased to 32.1 bushels per acre. At the present time the average yield is over 40 bushels, and yields of 100 bushels an acre are common. [Carl L. Wilson, Walter E. Loomis, and Hannah T. Croasdale, *Botany*, 1972.]

Appearance order is that in which the writer seems to be describing a perception in an almost casual manner. Contrary to a first impression, however, this order is often difficult to handle, because the writer must follow a logical order while appearing to have no order. Otherwise, he may create nothing more than a hodgepodge of detail.

Appearance order is quite appropriate for such scenes as a real estate development. The writer first gives his overall impression (a large area of irregularly placed homes). He then recounts such facts as the varying shapes and sizes of buildings. Finally he proceeds to describe lawns, gardens, and similar details.

The greatest advantage of this approach is the appeal it derives from its apparently natural movement.

Below is a good example of appearance order.

- It was early evening of a day in the late fall and the Winesburg County Fair had brought crowds of country people into town. The day had been clear and the night came on warm and pleasant. On the Trunion Pike, where the road after it left town stretched away between berry fields now covered with dry brown leaves, the dust from passing wagons arose in clouds. Children, curled into little balls, slept on the straw scattered on wagon beds. Their hair was full of dust and their fingers black and sticky. The dust rolled away over the fields and the departing sun set it ablaze with colors.

   In the main street of Winesburg crowds filled the stores and the side-walks. Night came on, horses whinnied, the clerks in the stores ran madly about, children became lost and cried lustily, an American town worked terribly at the task of amusing itself.   [Sherwood Anderson, "Sophistication," 1919.]

When using *space order* the writer organizes his material according to the location of each part in relation to those around it. For example, if a writer were to describe the sorting division of a large metropolitan post office, he could use this approach effectively. He would simply divide the entire floor area into small sectors and describe the activity within each one (first-class mail, parcel post, etc.) in order.

Below is an illustration of the space order approach. It describes what a famous English author sees from his Washington hotel window.

● I walk to the front window, and look across the road upon a long, straggling row of houses, one story high, terminating nearly opposite, but a little to the left, in a melancholy piece of waste ground with frowzy grass, which looks like a small piece of country that has taken to drinking, and has quite lost itself. Standing anyhow and all wrong, upon this open space, like something meteoric that has fallen down from the moon, is an odd, lop-sided, one-eyed kind of wooden building, that looks like a church, with a flag-staff as long as itself sticking out of a steeple something larger than a tea-chest. Under the window, is a small stand of coaches, whose slave-drivers are sunning themselves on the steps of our door, and talking idly together. The three most obtrusive houses near at hand are the three meanest. On one—a shop, which never has anything in the window, and never has the door open—is painted in large characters, "The City Lunch." At another, which looks like the backway to somewhere else, but is an independent building in itself, oysters are procurable in every style. At the third, which is a very, very little tailor's shop, pants are fixed to order; or, in other words, pantaloons are made to measure. And that is our street in Washington.   [Charles Dickens, *American Notes*, 1842.]

The following passage illustrates the space order approach employed to describe a general—as opposed to a specific—situation. In this selection, the author is discussing the steamboat of the last century.

● . . . the main part of the western steamboat cabin consisted of a long and narrow saloon flanked on each side by a row of staterooms. At the forward end of the saloon on either side in line with staterooms were the clerk's office and the bar. Before the introduction of the Texas, the quarters of the captain and pilots as well as the clerk were usually located in the forward part of the cabin. Washrooms, barbershop, nursery, pantry, kitchen, and various service rooms usually found a place adjacent to the wheelhouses on either side of the boat on the cabin deck or immediately below.   [Louis C. Hunter, *Steamboats on the Western Rivers: An Economic and Technological History*, 1949.]

Exposition

Because of the basic purpose of exposition—to explain a process, function, thought, or institution—the matter of organization is especially important. The entire work must be so organized that it leads the reader unerringly from point to point, eventually giving him a thoroughly clear understanding of the writer's every thought.

The primary fact about the organization of expository writing is that it has the usual three divisions found in most writing— introduction, body, and conclusion.

The *introduction* sets the stage. It gives the reader a perspective on the question, on the writer's view of the subject, and on the organization of the entire work. In addition, it should serve to create interest.

The selection below introduces Cardinal Newman's well known defense of himself, his actions, and his church after prolonged attacks by his enemies. Newman had renounced Protestantism almost 20 years before to enter the Roman Catholic Church.

● It may easily be conceived how great a trial it is to me to write the following history of myself; but I must not shrink from the task. The words "Secretum meum mihi," keep ringing in my ears; but as men draw towards their end, they care less for disclosures. Nor is it the least part of my trial, to anticipate that my friends may, upon first reading what I have written, consider much in it irrelevant to my purpose; yet I cannot help thinking that, viewed as a whole, it will effect what I wish it to do.   [John Henry Newman, "Apologia Pro Vita Sua," 1864.]

Below are two introductions to well known works.

● Over increasingly large areas of the United States, spring now comes unheralded by the return of the birds, and the early mornings are strangely silent where once they were filled with the beauty of bird song. This sudden silencing of the song of birds, this obliteration of the color and beauty and interest they lend to our world have come about swiftly, insidiously, and unnoticed by those whose communities are as yet unaffected. [Rachel Carson, *Silent Spring*, 1962.]

• Of all literary forms the book review is the one most widely cultivated and least often esteemed. To many the very phrase "literary form" may smack of pretense when applied to a kind of writing which is usually so casual; and formlessness may, indeed, be the only form of many commentaries on books. Book reviewing can, nevertheless, become an art in itself and would be such more often if the ambitious reviewer would only devote himself to the cultivation of its particular excellences instead of attempting, as he so often does, to demonstrate his capacities by producing something "more than a mere review." The best review is not the one which is trying to be something else. It is not an independent essay on the subject of the book in hand and not an aesthetic discourse upon one of the literary genres. The best book review is the best review of the book in question, and the better it is the closer it sticks to its ostensible subject. [Joseph Wood Krutch, "What Is a Good Review?" *The Nation*, April 1937.]

In expository writing, the *body* is the part that presents the bulk of the message. It, therefore, is the section that is most extensive, most demanding, and most important.

The organization of the body is influenced by (1) the number of points to be discussed, (2) the extent to which each point is to be developed, and (3) the complexity of each point. Although these considerations are self-evident, they must be stressed because the writer must make important decisions regarding especially the second and third considerations. He must decide how extensively to discuss each point and how deeply to probe the complexities involved.

The function of the conclusion in expository writing is to make a statement of summation and to leave the reader with a strong dominant impression. This point can be illustrated by citing the three conclusions quoted below.

● If the freshman will take advantage of his adviser's experience, of his teachers' knowledge and of the wealth of his college library, and if he will study on his own, most of his minor adjustment problems will disappear. He will stop thinking of the college degree as a high-class work permit, a ticket of admission to this or that job. He will know that hard, analytical study is required in college. He will realize that liberal education means a good balance between academic, athletic, and social life. And he will surely, out of his broad background, find a special interest to develop into a college major, even if it turns out to be an "impractical" field like Chinese, Indic philology or archaeology.

And the man or woman who finds out what education means has grown up. Surely the proof of the broad education which Americans can get if they want it is a deep understanding of how good that education can be.   [Robert U. Jameson, "How to Stay in College," *Saturday Evening Post*, 1954.]

● But liberal education must so educate the individual that he is manifestly worthy of having his dignity recognized. If he wishes to lead his fellows, he must first learn to lead himself. Without education for privacy he will neither merit leadership nor learn to recognize it in others. He will strive in vain for happiness and success in private or public life until he has achieved understanding, goodness, serenity, and contentment within himself. That, according to my exegesis, is in this connection the meaning of the Biblical text: "For what is a man profited, if he shall gain the whole world, and lose his own soul?" It is surely what Thomas Hardy meant when he wrote:

He who is with himself dissatisfied,
Though all the world find satisfaction in him,
Is like a rainbow-coloured bird gone blind,
That gives delight it shares not.

[Marten Ten Hoor, "Education for Privacy," *American Scholar*, 1955.]

● The result, as Robert Schrank of Mobilization for Youth has written, is that the life history of teenage slum dwellers has been "a continuum of failure." Lower-class dropouts, particularly Negroes and Puerto Ricans, "do not want to fail," Schrank argues, "and yet they know nothing else." This affects the youngsters' ability to perform on the job as well as in school. For the dropouts, as Schrank puts it, "have been conditioned to the idea that they are stupid." More important, they "have been conditioned to feel they are not capable of solving problems"; anything that smacks of problem-solving brings back what Schrank aptly terms "the reflex of failure." In sum, academic failure reinforces the slum youngster's sense of being trapped by an alien and hostile world, and persuades him that there is no way—certainly no legitimate way—for one of his background or skin color to "make it" in the world at large.   [Charles E. Silberman, "What Hit the Teenagers," *Fortune*, April 1965.]

To illustrate the process of organizing material for an expository writing, let us assume that a writer is going to explain the need for a uniform code to license operators of motor vehicles. As he reflects, he obtains the following thoughts.

present system is on a state to state basis

system varies sharply from state to state

difference in minimum age requirement. Some states have minimum age as low as 15; others, as high as 18.

differences in minimum age for type of vehicle to be driven (family car, truck, school bus, etc.)

physical requirements vary from state to state. Some have only a test for vision; others have more requirements.

some states issue a permanent license. Others require periodic examinations after a stipulated age (usually 50).

present system is dangerous because it does not keep abreast of mechanical changes in cars (e.g., stick shift to automatic transmission)

present system is actually licensing incompetent people to drive cars under any conditions (e.g., anyone can drive in any kind of storm or any kind of difficult traffic situation such as rush hour traffic on main arteries)

present tests are frequently not simulated to actual conditions of highways (e.g., high speed travel on turnpikes)

no uniform laws for suspension of driver's privileges for infractions

no widespread reciprocal agreement of states regarding suspended licenses

accidents frequently caused by incompetent drivers who cannot be held responsible (e.g., elderly drivers in tunnels often cause chain reaction collisions by slowing down suddenly, but their cars are not touched. Hence they are not considered "involved.")

situation is fast approaching chaos

After the writer has listed all the pertinent thoughts, he then turns to the preparation of the outline from which to do his actual writing. Below is an outline constructed for the thoughts presented above.

The Need for Uniform Laws
to License Operators of Motor Vehicles

I. Introduction
   A. Present system characterized by inconsistencies, laxities, and potential dangers
   B. Situation becoming worse daily
   C. Immediate remedial action needed

II. Body
   A. Present system under control of individual states
   B. Requirements vary on basic matters
      1. Minimum age
      2. Physical aptitude
      3. Nature of actual test
      4. Length of validity period of license
   C. Dangerous implications of present system
      1. Tests fail to evaluate ability to drive a variety of vehicles under a variety of conditions

2. Tests not simulated to actual road conditions
3. Present systems frequently take no cognizance of loss of aptitude with age

III. Conclusion
    A. A matter for the attention of all citizens
    B. Remedial action imperative

Argument

The primary purpose of argument is to persuade or to convince. Hence, when you attempt to persuade another or others to accept a conclusion or a viewpoint, you are engaging in argument.

The guiding principle in the organization of argument rests on one consideration: how can the individual points be arranged to obtain maximum impact? In some cases, the strongest argument should be presented first. In other instances, it may be most potent when placed last. On still other occasions, you may see fit to intersperse stronger arguments with weaker ones.

To illustrate the problem, a representative situation can be used. Let us assume that an argument is to be prepared advocating higher salaries for local police officers. The three principal arguments are:

1. Local officers are currently receiving salaries below the national average for their positions.

2. Higher salaries are needed to hold and attract persons of high calibre.

3. Higher salaries are needed to ensure the morale necessary for an efficient police department.

Most persons would probably agree that of the three arguments, the first carries least weight. If advanced first, the advantage of a strong beginning is lost. If saved for last, the impact of a strong ending is sacrificed. Naturally, no final statement can be made in this instance; each writer must decide for himself. Yet generally speaking, most capable writers of argument prefer to lead with their strongest argument. To counteract the tapering-off effect caused by this arrangement, they usually attempt to close with a strong conclusion.

The organization of material for argument employs the introduction, body, and conclusion used in expository writing.

The introduction in argument sets the stage for the material that follows. It prepares the reader for your main points and your approach in establishing those points.

Below are three representative introductions to various kinds of argument.

- Were it not for the twin forces of curiosity and discontent, man would still be living in caves and brush shelters, inadequately clad in crude skins and nourished by half-burned, half-cooked gobbets of whatever animals he managed to kill with the crudest, stone-tipped weapons. Curiosity is not unique to man, but man alone fortified it with speculation and the capacity for symbolic projection, so that he could wonder "why," and "what would happen if..." Without it, it is doubtful if we should even have religion. [Oliver La Farge, "The Art of Discontent," 1952.]

- Of dictionaries, as of newspapers, it might be said that the bad ones are too bad to exist, the good ones too good not to be better. No dictionary of a living language is perfect or ever can be, if only because the time required for compilation, editing, and issuance is so great that shadows of obsolescence are falling on parts of any such work before it ever gets into the hands of the user. Preparation of *Webster's Third New International Dictionary of the English Language* began intensively in the Springfield establishment of G. & C. Merriam Company in 1936, but the century was nine months into its seventh decade before any outsider could have his first look at what had been accomplished. His first look is, of course, incompetent to acquaint him with the merits of the new work; these no one can fully discover without months or years of everyday use. On the other hand, it cost only minutes to find out that what will rank as the great event of American linguistic history in the decade, and perhaps in this quarter century, is in many crucial particulars a very great calamity.   [Wilson Follett, "Sabotage in Springfield," *The Atlantic*, January 1962.]

- The storm of abuse in the popular press that greeted the appearance of *Webster's Third New International Dictionary* is a curious phenomenon. Never has a scholarly work of this stature been attacked with such unbridled fury and contempt. An article in the *Atlantic* viewed it as a "disappointment," a "shock," a "calamity," "a scandal and a disaster." The New York *Times*, in a special editorial, felt that the work would "accelerate the deterioration" of the language and sternly accused the editors of betraying a public trust. The *Journal* of the American Bar Association saw the publication as "deplorable," "a flagrant example of lexicographic irresponsibility," "a serious blow to the cause of good English." *Life* called it "a non-word deluge," "monstrous," "abominable," and "a cause for dismay." They doubted that "Lincoln could have modelled his Gettysburg Address" on it—a concept of how things get written that throws very little light on Lincoln but a great deal on *Life*.

  What underlies all this sound and fury? Is the claim of the G. & C. Merriam Company, probably the world's greatest dictionary maker, that the preparation of the work cost $3.5 million, that it required the efforts of three hundred scholars over a period of twenty-seven years, working on the largest collection of citations ever assembled in any language—is all this a fraud, a hoax?

  So monstrous a discrepancy in evaluation requires us to examine basic principles. Just what's a dictionary for? What does it propose to do? What does the common reader go to a dictionary to find? What has the purchaser of a dictionary a right to expect for his money?   [Bergen Evans, "But What's a Dictionary For?" *The Atlantic*, May 1962.]

The body of argument, like the body of all other types of writing, conveys the bulk of the message. It presents the writer's main points and develops them with the aim of persuading the reader to accept his viewpoint or central thought.

The conclusion then attempts to draw together all the writer's principal thoughts in order to leave a dominant idea in the mind of the reader. The conclusion, therefore, is successful in direct proportion to its ability to make a statement of summation and to place within the reader's consciousness a strong dominant thought.

Below are three representative conclusions to pieces of writing that are basically arguments.

- The history of photography has been less a journey than a growth. Its movement has not been linear and consecutive, but centrifugal. Photography, and our understanding of it, has spread from a center; it has, by infusion, penetrated our consciousness. Like an organism, photography was born whole. It is in our progressive discovery of it that its history lies.   [John Szarkowski, *The Photographer's Eye*, 1966.]

- Thus, if we could discover a purely poetic and purely practical person, might they reason together. But we can discover nothing so satisfactory to our definitions, and therefore let us conclude the discussion of the difference between them. It has led us to our own end—a clearer understanding of the nature of poetic people, and of all people when they are in the poetic mood. They are lovers of the qualities of things. They are not engaged, as the learned say that all life is, in becoming acquainted with it. They are possessed by the impulse to realize, an impulse as deep, and arbitrary, and unexplained as that "will to live" which lies at the bottom of all explanations. It seems but the manifestation, indeed, of that will itself in a concrete and positive form. It is a wish to experience life and the world. That is the essence of the poetic temper.   [Thomas De Quincey, "Literature of Knowledge and Literature of Power," 1891.]

- That man, I think, has had a liberal education who has been so trained in youth that his body is the ready servant of his will, and does with ease and pleasure all the work that, as a mechanism, it is capable of; whose intellect is a clear, cold, logic engine, with all its parts of equal strength, and in smooth working order; ready, like a steam engine, to be turned to any kind of work, and spin the gossamers as well as forge the anchors of the mind; whose mind is stored with a knowledge of the great and fundamental truths of nature and of the laws of her operations; one who, no stunted ascetic, is full of life and fire, but whose passions are trained to come to heel by a vigorous will, the servant of a tender conscience; who learned to love all beauty, whether of nature or of art, to hate all vileness, and to respect others as himself.

Such a one and no other, I conceive, has had a liberal education; for he is, as completely as a man can be, in harmony with nature. He will make the best of her, and she of him. They will get on together rarely; she as his ever-beneficent mother; he as her mouthpiece, her conscious self, her minister and interpreter. [Thomas Henry Huxley, "A Liberal Education and Where to Find It," 1948.]

16.

From rough draft to final copy

When you first begin to write, watch for the times when you can compose with maximum facility and competence and try to use this time for all your writing.

Some few people, it seems, can write well at almost any hour of the day or night. For most, however, one time is better than another. Generally, most of us do our best when we are most calm, rested, and free of pressures. This time is usually the daylight or early evening hours.

Also, try to find a quiet, comfortable place to work. Beware colorful stories of famous writers at work. Thomas Wolfe sometimes did walk the streets in the early morning hours to reflect on his material. Fine short stories have been written in cafes and assorted hangouts. Yet, most writers have worked in glamorless settings—in a workaday fashion. This, then, will probably be your lot also.

Writing the rough draft

Before beginning to write your first draft, you should study at length your outline and general plan of attack. This will refresh your memory and give you a tighter sense of direction. Further, it will enable you to consider once more the relative importance of your points; that is, it will help to prevent the danger of overdeveloping one point at the expense of another.

When you work on your first draft, aim for high-quality writing. The belief that a writer can express himself loosely on the first writing because it is only a rough casting has serious weaknesses. A draft conceived in this manner often represents wasted time. The word choice is likely to be so broad, the expression so rambling, and the style so loose that the work becomes little more than verbose conversation. The writer, like the sprinter who jumps the gun, has made a false start.

Most people's reluctance to consign any writing to the waste-basket leads to an attempt to polish badly designed, poorly executed sentences when beginning again would be more profitable. So, given a loose first draft, the writer often struggles fruitlessly against bad writing—thereby wasting time and effort on a product well below the level of his best work.

Equally important, guard against factual errors, misspellings, and similar shortcomings in your rough draft. The many reasons why such errors should be avoided include the following:

A factual error detected after completion of the first draft often necessitates a serious rewriting of the entire work.

A misspelling not corrected on the first draft often appears in the final draft.

Mentally noted corrections are often forgotten under the pressure of making the final copy.

Any postponements made in the checking of facts increase the chances that the checking will never be done.

Revising for the final copy

As you set out to revise your rough draft, you are engaging in a crucial procedure. You are casting your composition into its final form; you are establishing the final quality of your writing. Therefore, you must labor at your highest level of care and competence.

As you revise, your primary function is to give finish or polish to your writing, that is, to improve the whole undertaking.

To polish your writing, you should proceed as if you were attempting to improve the writing of another person. Thinking in terms of the desirable qualities already discussed, examine every sentence carefully in the hope of strengthening it. Also, watch for the opportunity to introduce any especially useful stylistic device listed in preceding chapters.

Further, as you revise, visualize yourself as an editor. Check for vague or clouded expression; be wary of errors in mechanics; seek at every turn the atmosphere of finished craftsmanship.

In the revision stage, certain guidelines merit any writer's attention. First and especially significant is the necessity of time lapses. Most writers can revise their work best when they allow a day or two between the completion of the rough draft and the first editing and between the first and second editings. The intervening time provides a clearer perspective and a greater sense of objectivity; it enables the writers to view their work with a greater sense of detachment. In fact, these "no contact" periods sometimes give them the feeling that they are examining their work for the first time. They are better able to detect weak sentence structure, clouded expression, mechanical errors, and other shortcomings.

Second, as you reread your sentences in the rough draft, you should ask yourself two questions: Have I said what I mean? Do I mean what I say? Even though they appear to be almost too elementary to ask, these questions are quite complex and their answers provide a sure guide to clarity of expression. If you can answer each question with a clear affirmative, you have stated your thoughts clearly.

Third, you must remember effective writing "reads itself." This statement means that as you read a paragraph or longer passage, you should feel a certain smoothness, a certain rhythm, a certain perfection of expression that creates an appealing natural momentum. This momentum seems to carry you along in the manner of the swimmer moving with the tide. In fact, in the best of writing, this momentum has a magnetic quality; it draws the reader from sentence to sentence.

The fact that good writing reads itself makes the task of revising quite difficult. You must often rework your phraseology, invert your sentences, and strive for smooth transitions for hours on end before obtaining the effect desired. Yet each time that you succeed, you can be certain that you have strengthened your ability in this area.

To appreciate the power of an appealing sentence rhythm, you need only think of famous lines, such as those presented below, and the pleasure you felt when you first met them.

- These are the times that try men's souls. [Thomas Paine, "The Crisis," 1776.]

- With malice toward none; with charity for all; with firmness in the right, as God gives us to see the right, let us strive on to finish the work we are in; to bind up the nation's wounds; to care for him who shall have borne the battle, and for his widow, and his orphan—to do all which may achieve and cherish a just and lasting peace among ourselves, and with all nations. [Abraham Lincoln, "Second Inaugural Address," 1865.]

To appreciate the presence of appealing rhythm in longer passages, you need only examine selections such as the ones that follow. The first is by a college freshman; the second is by Joseph Addison, one of the great stylists of all time. In the first selection, you can easily note the labored effect, the grinding, and the abrupt transitions. In the second, there is an ease of execution that makes the writing read itself, thereby creating an overall quality of appeal and strength.

- The river seemed to be a mass of churning water. There were three or four merchant ships moving down the stream. We could see a bridge through the haze in the distance. Across the other side of the river was a row of little shacks used by neighboring people as boat houses. The houses were all shapes and sizes. We thought that they looked very strange because they seemed to be rather badly cared for.

    As we sat there looking at the shacks, a large tug came

plowing through the waves. It seemed bent on reaching its destination in a big hurry. It kept going until it reached a spot about 400 yards up the river. Then it stopped, turned, and pressed itself against the side of a huge barge. Another tug came in on the other side of the barge, and the two tugs began to push the barge down the river.

● As Sir Roger is landlord to the whole congregation, he keeps them in very good order, and will suffer nobody to sleep in it besides himself; for, if by chance he has been surprised into a short nap at sermon, upon recovering out of it he stands up and looks about him, and if he sees anybody else nodding, either wakes them himself, or sends his servant to them. Several other of the old knight's particularities break out upon these occasions; sometimes he will be lengthening out a verse in the Singing-Psalms half a minute after the rest of the congregation have done with it; sometimes, when he is pleased with the matter of his devotion, he pronounces "Amen" three or four times to the same prayer; and sometimes stands up when everybody else is upon their knees, to count the congregation, or see if any of his tenants are missing.

I was yesterday very much surprised to hear my old friend, in the midst of the service, calling out to one John Matthews to mind what he was about and not disturb the congregation. This John Matthews, it seems, is remarkable for being an idle fellow, and at that time was kicking his heels for his diversion. This authority of the knight, though exerted in that odd manner which accompanies him in all circumstances of life, has a very good effect upon the parish, who are not polite enough to see anything ridiculous in his behavior; besides that the general good sense and worthiness of his character make his friends observe these little singularities as foils that rather set off than blemish his good qualities.

As soon as the sermon is finished nobody presumes to stir till Sir Roger is gone out of the church. The knight walks down from his seat in the chancel between a double row of his tenants, that stand bowing to him on each side, and every now and then inquires how such an one's wife, or mother, or son, or father do, whom he does not see at church—which is understood as a secret reprimand to the person that is absent.   [Joseph Addison, *The Spectator*, 1711.]

Fourth, as you reread your own work, you must not fall into the trap of assuming that because a sentence is clear to you, it is automatically clear to someone else. This pitfall exists because as anyone reads his own writing, he feels his own style; he hears his own voice as he reads, and he gives intonations and stresses that play a dominant role in establishing meaning. Thus, idiosyncrasies of sentence structure, cumbersome phraseology, and involved patterns of expression disappear for the writer—but remain for the reader.

Fifth, you must recognize the dangers of seeking assistance from a second person. Quite often, beginning writers rely on the help of friends and others to "dress up" their writing or to check for errors in spelling and other mechanics.

The great danger of such assistance is that the work may become a joint effort, thereby depriving the writer of the opportunity of producing a work all his own. His composition becomes somewhat like the portrait that the art teacher touches up for the student painter. It becomes a two-person product that reflects, however gently, two personalities.

To illustrate the entire process of revising a rough copy, the student writing below is presented. Note especially the attempts to obtain a smoother, more pointed expression. Also, study carefully the comments on the revisions.

●   *Man's Greatest Asset*

　　　　　　　　　　　　　his
1　　Man's greatest asset is ~~the~~ ability to think logically.

　　　　　　　　　　　civilization, man has employed various
2　Since the beginning of ~~mankind, problems have been solved by~~

　　　forms of logic to solve his problems and through this process
3　~~the use of logical deduction. The knowledge which has been~~

　　　has achieved gains that are almost
4　~~gained by this particular method of thinking is~~ beyond ~~one's~~

5 From the first
comprehension. ~~To think that man first started with very~~

6 the and the man has learned to
crude instruments such as ~~a~~ knife ~~or~~ spearhead, ~~and today we~~

7 and to
build rockets that ~~will~~ fly to the moon unmanned, ~~or we can~~

8 unleash enormous amounts of energy from splitting the atom. ~~is~~

9 like
~~startling.~~ Without the ability to think logically ~~such~~ men ~~as~~

10 never have developed the/
Michelangelo, Newton, Einstein could ~~not bring their~~ ideas ~~forth~~

11 that form the basis for and
~~about~~ flying, calculus, ~~or~~ atomic energy. ~~because they would not~~

12 ~~be able to conceive how anything could fly or how one would solve~~

13 ~~a complicated problem, or know that energy is equal to the proper-~~

14 ~~ties that Einstein says it equals.~~

15 still
If it had not been for logical deduction, we would be living

16 ~~in this year 1972~~ in caves. But God has given man the ability to

17 , and man has used it with considerable success. Among
think logically/ ~~And because of this great asset, man has created~~

18 other achievements, he has created/ —
a society that is highly sophisticated/ ~~The human race has~~

19 because of
~~built~~ a society where life becomes easier every day ~~due to~~

20 labor saving devices. Man's use of logic has also contributed greatly
~~the fact that men are producing machines which do the work~~

21 to increasing life expectancy through
~~for us. The life expectancy of a person is rapidly rising~~

22 conducted
~~because of the~~ research ~~being done~~ in the field of medicine.

Comments

Line 1
"His" makes the sentence more pointed. It creates a note of definiteness to the statement.

Line 2
"Civilization" is more precise because, technically speaking, "mankind" began with the earliest form of Homo sapiens, who lived as an animal. Obviously, in such a situation, there is a strong question concerning the use of deductive logic to solve problems. The shift to active voice makes the sentence stronger.

Lines 2-5
The expression has been made more pointed and hence more effective. Note especially the efforts to make it more concise.

Line 6
"The" makes the thought more concrete. "And" must replace "or" in the interests of accuracy of meaning. "The" must be placed before "spearhead" to gain a parallel construction. Note also the improvement in the rhythm of the sentence.

Line 7
"Will" must be deleted because the present tense is required. "And" is needed for accuracy.

Line 9
The deletions make the line more concise.

Line 10
The original tense was incorrect.

Lines 11-14
The great number of words first used created a note of verbosity. No significant element of thought was lost in making the sentence more concise.

Lines 15-16
The revision has made the expression more concise. It has also removed a slight possibility of "dating" the writing.

Line 17
The revised expression is more concise, more precise, and hence more pointed.

Line 18
The use of the appositive aids in gaining sentence variety and giving a more pleasing rhythm to the sentence.

Line 19
Most authorities on usage prefer "because of" to "due to" in this instance.

Lines 20-22
The recast version makes the sentences and total expression more concise, precise, and pointed.

Appendix: Rules for the use of the comma

1. The comma is used at the end of the first independent clause in the compound sentence.

- Jim stayed home, but I went to work.
- The captain issued the order, and the crew moved to their assignments.

2. The comma is used to separate the dependent from the independent clause in the complex sentence if the dependent clause comes first.

- If Joe is there, ask him to help.
- When Kim returns, give him this package.
- Ask Joe to help if he is there.
- Give Kim this package when he returns.

Note: if the writer desires to emphasize a dependent clause that does not precede an independent clause, he may use a comma to gain the emphasis.

- Ask Joe to help, if he is there.
- Give Kim this package, when he returns.

3. The comma is used in a series of three or more items to separate each item.

● He needs paper, ink, pencils, and clips.
● He was tired, weary, and depressed.

Note: some authorities in usage state that the last comma (the one before the "and") may be omitted. However, such an omission may create a vague or unsettled meaning. What, for example, are the three items in the following series?

We spoke to the President, Vice President and Secretary and Treasurer.

4. The comma is used to separate unrelated adjectives. (Adjectives are unrelated when each modifies the same noun independently.)

● He is a steady, consistent worker.
● It was a long, hard job.

Note: the adjectives in the sentence below are not separated from each other because they are related adjectives. Notice how "new" in the first sentence modifies both "cleaner" and "vacuum cleaner."

● Mother bought a new vacuum cleaner.
● Mrs. Greenberg has a hammered silver tray.

A helpful guide: to test whether the comma belongs or not, simply substitute the word "and" for the comma. If you have used the comma correctly, the sentence reads smoothly.

5. The comma is used to set off the nonrestrictive clause. (A

nonrestrictive clause is one that does not restrict the subject in any way.)

- John, who is my brother, likes apple pie.
- The car, which is certainly flashy, is a 1974 model.

Note: no commas are used in the following sentences because the clauses within the sentence are restrictive; that is, they restrict the subject.

- Students who earn all A's are rare.
- The tickets that have perforated edges are for the reserved section.

A helpful guide: when a nonrestrictive clause is removed from the sentence, no change occurs in the basic meaning of the sentence. When a restrictive clause is removed, a totally different meaning results.

6. The comma is used to set off the appositive.

- Mr. Jackson, the head teller, entered the bank.
- The prairie dog, a small rodent, is a real nuisance.

7. The comma is used to ensure clarity.

- Outside, the wind was howling furiously.
- Below, the water was rough and menacing.
- For John, Paul Jones was a real friend.

8. The comma is used in direct address to set off nouns and pronouns.

- Merriam, keep your eye on the ball.
- You, you, and you, now is the time to act.

- Here, Jim, is the book you want.

9. The comma is used to set off the participial phrase.

- Leaving his competitors far behind, Secretariat won easily.
- Secretariat, leaving his competitors far behind, won easily.
- Secretariat won easily, leaving his competitors far behind.

10. The comma is used to set off a contrasting element.

- The right foot, never the left, is used on this pedal.
- Mr. Clayborne, not Mr. Claywell, is the chairman.

11. The comma is used to set off the absolute element.

- The sun setting behind us, we pushed on across the gulch.
- Her head high, the filly rounded the first turn.
- The filly, her head high, rounded the first turn.

12. The comma is used to set off the parenthetical element.

- Our neighbor's cat, bless his ornery soul, walked across the freshly painted porch.
- The Rolls-Royce, what a car that was, is gone from the scene.

13. The comma is used to denote omissions.

- Jake won 3 games; Pete, 4; and Lou, 8.

14. The comma is used to separate the elements within the total unit of a date or place.

- Barbara was born on Tuesday, July 3, 1952, in Traynor, Pike County, Wisconsin, of French parentage.

Catalog

If you are interested in a list of fine Paperback
books, covering a wide range of subjects
and interests, send your name and address,
requesting your free catalog, to:

McGraw-Hill Paperbacks
1221 Avenue of Americas
New York, N.Y. 10020